A Dream Worth Fighting For

A DREAM

WORTH FIGHTING FOR

Never Let Obstacles Stop You from Being Your Best Self

TIM HIGHTOWER
WILLIAM L. SACHS

NEW YORK

LONDON • NASHVILLE • MELBOURNE • VANCOUVER

A DREAM WORTH FIGHTING FOR

Never Let Obstacles Stop You from Being Your Best Self

Published in New York, New York, by Morgan James Publishing. Morgan James is a trademark of Morgan James, LLC. www.MorganJamesPublishing.com

Scripture taken from the NEW KING JAMES VERSION (NKJV)®. Copyright© 1982 by Thomas Nelson, Inc. Used by permission. All rights reserved

Proudly distributed by Ingram Publisher Services.

Morgan James BOGO™

A **FREE** ebook edition is available for you or a friend with the purchase of this print book.

_____

CLEARLY SIGN YOUR NAME ABOVE

Instructions to claim your free ebook edition:
1. Visit MorganJamesBOGO.com
2. Sign your name CLEARLY in the space above
3. Complete the form and submit a photo of this entire page
4. You or your friend can download the ebook to your preferred device

ISBN 9781631957703 paperback
ISBN 9781631957710 ebook
Library of Congress Control Number:
2022934165

Cover Design by:
Emmanuel L. Hightower
Creative Director at Lion Vision Group

Interior Design by:
Chris Treccani
www.3dogcreative.net

Morgan James is a proud partner of Habitat for Humanity Peninsula and Greater Williamsburg. Partners in building since 2006.

Get involved today! Visit MorganJamesPublishing.com/giving-back

To my parents, Lewis and Nikkie Hightower, you gave me love, support, and a strong sense of purpose. I love you.

In loving memory of Elizabeth Austin Tucker
"Nothing shall separate us from the love of God"

Table of Contents

Chapter One	On a Sunny Afternoon in Charlotte	1
Chapter Two	The Decision	13
Chapter Three	Who Would Have Imagined?	25
Chapter Four	Twists and Turns in Maryland	37
Chapter Five	Entering a New World	49
Chapter Six	Don't Tell Me What I Can't Do	63
Chapter Seven	One Duffle Bag	75
Chapter Eight	Use What Got You Here	87
Chapter Nine	Change or Remain the Same?	99
Chapter Ten	Losing Myself	111
Chapter Eleven	In a Vulnerable Place	123
Chapter Twelve	See Me for Who I Am	137
Chapter Thirteen	Consider the Cost	151
Chapter Fourteen	Prepare As If	165
Chapter Fifteen	Seeking and Finding	179
Acknowledgments		*193*
About the Authors		*197*

Chapter One

ON A SUNNY AFTERNOON IN CHARLOTTE

"Tim, wake up, wake up."

The voice hits me like the clanging of an alarm clock. But it isn't morning, it is afternoon, isn't it? For an instant, it's not clear. All of a sudden there are only questions with no answers. What's happening? I am not sure. It feels like a dream. But not a good dream. Things aren't going well. Something's not right. Why am I lying on the ground?

Pain shoots through my left leg. I try to move, but it hurts, all around the knee. No wonder I'm lying on the ground. But wait. How did I get there? Did anyone tackle me? I open my eyes and see a football nearby. Was it a fumble? I pound the ground in frustration with my fist. How could I fumble, and not remember? Nobody touched me. What happened?

Time to motivate myself. Come on, Tim, get up. The demands on myself usually work. I do that all the time. But it's not working. In less than five seconds, I have gone from bliss, from being in the zone athletes crave, to confusion and pain. A pain that increases as the shock of being on the ground wears off.

My mind starts to regroup. OK, we're in Charlotte, North Carolina and this is the green grass of Bank of American Stadium. It is a crucial game. Impatience now. I know where I am. But people are telling me to get up. Now I'm angry. I try to get up, but I can't. More anger. I don't need help. I can do this. But things aren't working. And there is pain, incredible pain, in my left knee.

My determination stiffens. I won't acknowledge what's going on, because I don't know what's going on at all. Maybe I can convince them, maybe it's not that bad. My mind flies as my body struggles. But the pain won't go away. The left knee really hurts.

Let's sit up. It is not easy. When I finally do, there are players nearby, some taking a knee in prayer, some moving toward me. My mind ignites again, but I don't want to look at them. They must not see me like this. I feel weak, vulnerable. I do a quick review of my life, checking to see how things are going, as I have done for years. In an instant, memories of years of hard work and goals pursued flood back, especially the dream of becoming a professional football running back.

What did that dream mean? It meant feeling respected. Finding respect has been a goal that has driven my life. Now, I must be determined again, whatever this new challenge may be. I don't yet realize that it will take months and years to reach this new goal. The goal of dealing with what put me on the ground. My mind finds a familiar conviction and a new fear.

I want them to look up to me as a leader, as the hardest worker on the team. Now I am looking up to them, from the ground. I'm scared to show them that I don't have a clue. What just happened? What comes next?

It is quiet, even though 73,000 people are watching me lie on the ground. My Washington Redskins teammates whisper nervously as our opponents on this Sunday afternoon, the Carolina Panthers, watch silently. They all know that it could have happened to any of them. But this time it is my turn.

It is slowly dawning on me, as the voice becomes insistent. One of the team's trainers is yelling at me. "Tim wake up. We are going to have to call a cart for you." I respond loudly: "No, you're not." Insistence surges. "I walked onto this field on my own and I will walk off on my own." But could I?

Walking onto the field was not an issue earlier that afternoon. It was October 23, 2011, a promising day for the Washington Redskins of the National Football League, and for me, Tim Hightower, their starting running back. Going into this game Washington had three wins and two losses in prior games. A win in Charlotte would put us on track for a successful season and give us a chance to enter the playoff games. Success in those contests would lead to the pinnacle, the Super Bowl. I had been there as a member of the Arizona Cardinals. I was eager to return. The game in Charlotte would build momentum for a winning season.

I was primed for this game. I missed the previous game, against the Philadelphia Eagles, because of a sore shoulder. Our offense suffered, gaining only forty-two yards running with the ball, as we lost to the Eagles.

In the four games before Philadelphia, I had gained over two-hundred-thirty yards as one of several running backs. I had become the team's leading rusher and I was the starting running back against Carolina. In the first half, I gained nearly eighty yards carrying the ball. It was a great game. My role as a starter was coming together. The dream was coming true.

I was just beginning to scratch the surface of my potential. It was my fourth season in the NFL, the "contract year" players call it. If I completed four seasons with good performance, I could secure the long-term contract players dream of. It would secure my career and my future. This was the crucial year. I needed to prove myself in this fourth year, prove that I was a difference-maker on the field and a team leader in the locker room.

A veteran teammate had reminded me that there are only thirty-two starting running backs in the world, one for each NFL team. Sometimes I would think about the high school and college football running backs who dream of reaching where I had arrived. This was a rare opportunity and the crucial moment to achieve it. I wasn't going to let it go.

I had beaten incredible odds to make this dream come true. But I knew I had more to give, more ability to develop. Then it was Charlotte, and I was lying on the ground, not knowing what just happened. For the first time, in my dizzy state, I began to ask: what happens if everything I've prepared for is gone?

That question had never crossed my mind before, certainly not in the first half in Charlotte, even though Washington trailed Carolina 6–9 at halftime. But we seemed ready to take control of the game in the second half. For that to happen, my role was crucial. As the team prepared to leave the locker room and return to the field, Kyle Shanahan, my offensive coordinator, took me aside and looked me squarely in my face. "I'm putting this game on your shoulders," he told me. I was ready.

Few heard these words, but the message was clear: I had to take my game to another level. I was ready to continue doing what I had done in the first half, ready to lead Washington toward victory. It was the peak of football responsibility, everything I had dreamed of being and doing. I was well suited. Then everything fell apart.

Four minutes into the game's second half, the ball was handed off to me again. I had just made a first down and we were driving down the field toward a touchdown. No other player could match my running in that game. Not even close. But one play ended my game, stopped my career, and changed my life.

It happened in only a few seconds. I took the ball from our quarterback and secured it in my arms. Then I darted into an open area, our linemen having pushed Panther players aside. I don't always see the players around me, but I feel them. As I sped up, ready for another good gain, a Panther player appeared nearby. He lunged, his arms extended, trying to tackle me. I paused to evade this linebacker, planting my left leg to shift direction. But here my run ended.

When I planted my left leg, then twisted to change direction, the anterior cruciate ligament (ACL) in my left knee tore. I felt and heard a crack. It was horrible. I went down without an opposing player tackling me. Somehow, I held onto the ball, but the worst pain of my life began. It would not end soon. It was unlike anything I had ever felt before.

So, now, suddenly lying on the ground, stunned, in pain, dazed, bewildered, a new conversation starts within myself and with others. That conversation would redefine my life. Of course, that was not clear then, in the daze of injury. I did not know the lasting imprint of that new conversation, how my priorities and focus would change decisively. I would learn a new language and eventually be glad. But that lay in the future. First, I only want to get to my feet and get back into the game.

But that will not be easy. An unprecedented struggle has begun, involving a new focus and a new language of recovery from injury. Gradually it will become clear that recovery is a spiritual journey, featuring the demand of resilience, in soul and mind as well as in one's body. All of that would have made no sense until this moment, on this grass. At first, I would fight it, until recovery began to make sense, until resilience became my preoccupation. That would take time, four years to be exact.

I would wake up, but not only as the trainer's voice was insisting. I would wake up in terms of my life, in terms of all that matters to me. All the people who matter will matter more. I would understand my life and my faith in fulfilling ways as my recovery advanced. It was not easy, but this is the story I have to tell. It is a story of recovery and resilience. Of discovery and hard work and personal awakening.

I do not know much of this yet, lying on the grass in Charlotte. For now, figuring out what is going on and returning to the game are all that matter. I am the starter at running back. I intend to resume that role, as soon as possible. If that means going off the field briefly, I will do it. But I can hardly move. I go to take a step, and my knee gives out. All I can do is stop, take a deep breath, and feel confused. This is different, like nothing I have ever felt. I do not like it and want to get beyond it. There would be no easy answers.

The left knee not only hurts, but it is also unaccountably weak. I must hobble and don't like that one bit. It is not clear what's happening. Surely I can walk it off and dismiss those who want to help me off the field. I'm in pain, and I am pissed off. I can overcome it, whatever it is. So, I resist being assisted to the sidelines. I am fighting the reality that eventually I must face. I don't want help. I just want to get back into the game. It is what I had prepared for. Nothing can stand in my way. Nothing can diminish this determination.

Nevertheless, it takes assistance to get back to the team's bench. For a few minutes, I sit there in sullen silence. Already it seems as if my life is changing. But I won't acknowledge it. I vow that I will never give in. Even though I throw a towel over my face. Conviction and pain vie for attention in my mind. I am being tested in a new way, like I have never been tested before. This is all new. It has been forced upon me. There is no quick solution. It will only deepen, the extent of this injury testing the depth of my conviction for months to come.

The dread of total loss begins to creep into my mind. What if I can't come back to this game? What if I can't come back to football for a long time, or come back at all? What will I do if everything for which I prepared, for my entire life, suddenly is gone? What if my dream has been taken away in one instant, as my left knee cracked, and I went down? How will I respond? For the moment, I won't think about it, I can't answer. I hate even beginning to think like this. I was having a career day. Then it went away.

Until this moment, I had never been injured. Not like what this is becoming. This is new physical and mental territory and already I am fighting it. I had a stress fracture of a foot during my senior year at Episcopal High School. I had broken a thumb in 2009, during my second season in the NFL. Then I adjusted, missing some time, then playing through the healing. Of course, I will do that again, whatever this pain is. A quick adaptation and I will stay on course.

At first, I refuse the attempts of trainers to examine me. Sulking on the bench, towel over my face, comes first. A brief test of the knee brings more crunching and cracking and fresh pain. This thing is not going away. So, how do I get back into the game? So much depends on me. When trainers approach me, they are angrily waved off. But the pain persists, and the swelling is obvious.

It takes a while. I am still in competitive mode. Moving the knee is harder and more painful. Finally, I have to admit: something is not right. Gently a trainer approaches again. His voice is cautiously persistent. "We need to take a look at it." That need has become unavoidable.

It dawns on me, in agony on the sidelines, that I won't be going back into the game. It is the beginning of a mental shift as painful as the throbs from this knee. Something is wrong and it is bigger than I want to believe. This injury will keep me out, at least for the rest of this game. When the trainer tries to flex the knee, things get worse. I begin to grasp the situation.

Emotions flood me. Reality hits me. I think of the work I had done. The daily discipline. Training camp. Team meetings. Game preparation. The sore shoulder. The team lockout that suspended NFL play. The Arizona Cardinals had traded me to Washington in 2011. Does this injury prove they were right to let me go? Am I letting down Washington? Questions flood my mind. Each question has the same answer: my determination to succeed, to work harder than anyone else, to push through every obstacle. But this pain and this knee are different.

Yet I fight going to the locker room. There is something about going there; it is bad enough to be on the sidelines. My determination becomes intense, as pain turns to agony. The more the questions rise, the angrier I become. Too many questions, too few answers. I won't go anywhere without some answers. This was my time; I earned the right to be there. I won't let it go, regardless of what just happened. I can still hear Kyle

Shanahan's words, only a few minutes ago, in the locker room: "I'm putting this game on your shoulders." I will live up to it.

Now trainer after trainer tries to calm me down, but I won't listen. Players and staff also try. Then a veteran teammate approaches me. He puts his hand on my shoulder and says it will be OK. "We've got you," he says, "Your brothers got your back." After everything that has been said, and all the urgings of trainers, this is what I need to hear. Those words brought needed comfort. Someone has my back. I exhale and agree to do what is necessary. I will go to the locker room and let the trainers see what is going on in my left knee.

Looking back on this moment later, I realize those words triggered something in me. Up to that point, I put everything on my shoulders, just as the coach declared. I wanted responsibility, I thrived on it. More pressure meant more responsibility which equaled greater opportunity. If you don't experience pressure week in and week out, you're not a guy that teammates, coaches, family, and friends rely on. Delivering in the face of pressure created opportunities in high school, college, and then professionally.

Growing up I found strength from knowing my family was counting on me. In college, there was the time when my closest friend and teammate, Arman Shields, got hurt. We had trained together every day for four years. Each of us dreamed of playing in the NFL. Then, in the second game of the season, he hurt his knee. The look on his face spoke of hurt and disappointment. I knew it was bad. As a result, I felt a greater responsibility to succeed. I had a "career day," one of my best games in college football, and the next week as well. In a sense, I dedicated that college season to my friend. I credited Arman with much of my success. This was one of several memories now crowding my mind.

The Arizona Cardinals drafted me in 2008, giving me the chance to play professional football. But Washington gave me the responsibility I needed. A team only gives responsibility to a player whom they believe can truly lead them, on and off the field. I remember talking with the Cardinals' general manager before the 2011 season. I wanted more responsibility. I wanted to be the starting running back. I knew I could do it. If not with the Cardinals, then I wanted to go to a team where I could compete for a lead role. When the Cardinals traded me to Washington, I felt the responsibility I craved. My career was coming together. But as these memories shoot through my mind, I realize that my knee no longer is mine to control.

Finally, I agree to be carted off the bench to the locker room. Once there, I resign myself to the obvious. The team doctor examines me and frowns. The silence of trainers nearby tells the same story. I won't be going back to the field, not even to the bench. I was the starting running back. Now my game is over. Already I am afraid of an even worse outcome. What about the rest of the season? What about my career? My mind is a haze of pain, frustration, and dread. Who I am and what I had worked to build had come to a sudden halt. Was my life about to fall apart? I feel like a failure and hate it. All I can think about is that I am letting everybody down. Family, teammates, coaches. The people who were pulling for me, who counted on me to succeed, who believed in me as a running back and, more importantly, as a person.

There's something special about being a running back. It's a combination of skill, knowledge, and most of all toughness. I was always drawn to that position. A running back is the heart and soul of the offense. The running back can electrify a team, setting a pace, lifting them up. Running backs must do everything: run, catch passes, block, even throw passes on occasional trick plays. In the first half against Carolina, I carried the team and the coach put the game on my shoulders. A running back's performance can raise, or lower, the team. He sets a standard, an example. It is my ideal. It has been the goal, the source of incredible drive. Now, suddenly, when my team needs me, I can't deliver. I am in the locker room, injured. On the television there, I see my team is sinking. Carolina pulls ahead and remains ahead.

Suddenly there are noises. Someone is speaking loudly across the locker room. Voices raised in protest are ineffective; the man's voice is unrelenting. How he had gotten into the locker room never became clear. There were layers of security that should have barred him. But here he is, demanding loudly that no one could stop him from seeing his son. It is my father and now he is running toward me.

"Timothy? Where's my son," he demanded. My father comes running around the corner of a row of lockers. At that point, I can't hold back, my tears begin to fall. To this day I do not know how my father got into the locker room. But suddenly he is there, with the look of a man who is determined to get to his son. Being a father now I can understand the feeling. Then, my father begins to do what he often does, especially in a tense time: he prays. Now he prays for healing, for comfort, for strength. It is what I needed most, with my knee painful and swollen. It is a reminder that no matter how old, how tough, or how successful, a son never outgrows the need for his father's love. Instantly I go from being an angry, uncertain professional football player to a son who finds a moment's peace. I decide that I will face what I must face. It is a moment of faith. I find fresh motivation.

After praying, my father encourages me, as only a father can do. "I love you son. You're prepared. I put everything in you. You have to decide from here. I can't do it for you." That empowers me. It is exactly what I need to hear. "You have what it takes to get through this." I know that I will get through this and I feel grateful.

Chapter Two

THE DECISION

As a child, I didn't have much control over my living conditions. I felt defenseless as my family relocated from city to city, home to home. Sports provided an outlet and soon an identity. I could release frustration and build passion. Plus, I could feel control as my teammates depended on me to deliver in critical situations. The soul of an athlete was maturing within me, shaping who I was, pointing toward who I would become. It was thrilling.

When I reached the fourth grade, my soccer coach recommended that I play football. I tried it and immediately the position of running back was a natural fit. My father always recalled it differently. He would remind me that the first time I got hit as a football player I flinched and didn't like it. I was used to being bigger and stronger than all the soccer players and not being pushed around. Football was tougher, but it became my home. I knew it would be the moment I tried it. Playing football, even being injured, has shaped my life.

After getting over the idea of being hit and realizing that I could defend myself and hit back, I began to build confidence. Knowing that the ball would be in my hands play after play brought that feeling of excitement I wanted. It was a mentality, an athletic zone. I knew that I would get hit on every play. I learned that no matter how hard I got hit, I would get back up and do it again. Who would back down first, me or my opposition, would help to determine the outcome of a game. I learned to attack the defender, by strength as well as by feints. I began to seek dominance, to gain yards, and to score touchdown after touchdown.

My mind snaps back to the locker room in Charlotte where I am sitting. My confusion has eased. Prayer has worked, and pain-numbing medication helps. But my immobility is clear. It is also apparent, from distant rumbles, that the game has gone on without me. I watch a locker room television to see what I am missing. It is not good. By now the knee has some ice on it and a brace is being fitted. I have been propped up; I can't do it for myself. I hate it. I'm missing the action and immobilized. Frustration. It is the first of many times this reality sinks in.

I need to do something to make recovery happen. I text my personal trainer, in Arizona. Then I remember prior injuries. There was the broken thumb in my second season, as a Cardinal. I refused to go on the Injured Reserve list. A special cast had been created and I played with the Cardinals against Bret Favre and the Minnesota Vikings on Sunday night national television. Perhaps there could be a special cast for this knee now, regardless of how swollen, how painful, how much of a brace it would need. I can still play. I have to play.

I find momentary strength just from thinking about past times when I overcame what happened to me. But now the knee is throbbing, and I am still in the locker room and the game has moved on without me. It is becoming clear that this injury is different.

We lose the game to Carolina, 20–33. After Charlotte, our season stalls. From a record of three wins and two losses when we took the field in Charlotte, we finish the season with five wins and eleven losses. The Carolina game could have propelled us to a winning season, perhaps even the playoffs. Instead, the team would struggle, and I am on crutches, my future uncertain.

But I am determined to rally our team, just as I am trying to rally myself. Dad's talk inspired me. After the game, in the locker room, I speak to my teammates. On crutches, in a knee brace, pain winning over medication, I declare that I will fight and make it. They also must fight. They could overcome this day. We will stay together and move ahead. Determination challenges the gloom. It is a bitter day. But the team will turn it around, and I will be back.

I fly back to Washington on the team plane. It is a quiet flight, given the loss to the Panthers. There is little that anyone could say about the game. But while we are in the air, coaches and players slip back to my seat, my leg braced and stretched out. They express support. They reveal their respect for me. This leaves a huge, lasting memory. I had worked hard to be respected, as a person and as a player. But did it take an injury for me to feel, at last, something I had craved so deeply? The irony is striking. I got what I most needed and apparently lost it all at once. I become more determined. There is a lot to overcome. But I will do whatever is necessary.

When the team's plane lands at Dulles Airport, I am rushed off to a nearby hospital for x-rays and an MRI. Rikki, then my girlfriend, joins me. After I am examined, we wait. It would be the first of many times, facing things neither of us could control. Finally, late that night, the medical verdict arrives. A doctor comes out to explain, his face telling the story. It is bad. There is a severe ACL tear plus shaved bone. It is a severe injury and for the first time I hear the word "surgery." But I am not ready to hear that word, much less use it myself.

There is a roller-coaster of emotions. I am hurt. I know the knee is injured badly. But I cannot grasp the extent of this injury, physically or spiritually. The only thing on my mind is: when can I play again? At first, playing soon seems possible, in terms of what I hear from doctors and trainers. The doctor puts me on a regimen to prepare for knee surgery. But for me, it is a regimen to prepare for my return to the team. ASAP.

The regimen is designed to reduce the swelling of this knee, lessen the pain, and create as much range of motion as possible. I begin physical therapy at home and at the team's facility, coming and going on crutches. It hurts to see the team preparing for the next game without me. It hurts even more to see my replacement elevated to greater responsibility and status. That should be my role. I should be the starting running back. I worked hard. I earned it. The therapy is intended to prepare for knee surgery, but I have other ideas. The result is that I am working at odds with the medical professionals. I am obsessed: when will I play again? Will I ever be the same? Then I answer a phone call I never imagined I would receive.

A phone call from someone in the Washington organization was unlikely. As a player, I learned that if your phone rings after business hours and it is someone within the organization other than a coach, it only means one thing: your contract is being terminated. For some reason, when I saw the call came from the 703 area code, I was inclined to answer. The team's training facility has a 703 area-code phone listing. When I answered, I recognized the voice immediately.

"Hello Tim, this is Dan Snyder." Why would the owner of the Washington Redskins phone me at 9 PM? Immediately I felt relief. The owner would not phone to tell me I was being released from the team. That would be the role of a scout for the team. The relationship between player and owner was clear. Most players are aware of who the owner(s) are, but rarely if ever do they meet and speak with them. We play, they manage. That keeps emotions out of a working relationship. The distance between player and owner can be great. But it became close for a moment that night. This conversation was different.

"Tim, how are you doing?" he immediately asked. I told him I was OK, that the knee was strong. That I would be fine. I did not want to give him any reason for concern. I wanted to be positive. Was he phoning to find out how I was doing? Why did he phone? He quickly answered that question. "Tim, I'm sure you are nervous about your contract for next year. I know this is the last year of our contract with you. I just want you to know how we feel about you in this organization. We have seen how you carry yourself on the field and how you carry yourself off the field and in the community. We have noticed. You have been a leader for us. I want to tell you personally that we plan to sign you for next year. Focus on your recovery and do not worry about the business side."

I was speechless. I did not ask any questions. "OK, thank you, I will." That is all I could manage. Rikki, my fiancé, looked at me, trying to read the expression on my face. "What happened? What did he say?" For a minute I remained speechless.

My life had changed a few weeks earlier, all of a sudden, on the field in Charlotte. Now my life changed again. It seemed like an answer to prayer. Many decisions still lay ahead. But it felt good to have Dan Snyder's encouragement. That does not happen often, not from an owner. For the first time in weeks, Rikki and I smiled. Finally, some good news.

After the phone call from Dan Snyder, the decision seemed easy: I would have the knee surgery. It had not been so easy at first. I had never had surgery. I was worried about the impact on my career. My focus was on getting back onto the field as fast as possible. Now, something had come up that forced me to adapt, to do things differently. Still, with the team owner's encouragement, the decision seemed obvious. But it was not so easy. I was not certain my parents wanted me to have the knee surgery.

Time was ticking away. I had delayed the decision for a few weeks as I wrestled with this reality. I used the time to search every article I could find and to call every person I knew who had dealt with such an injury. I also phoned three doctors in the hope of a different opinion. At first, the more information I gathered, the more uncertain I became. Maybe Dan Snyder's call was a sign. For the first time in a while, I felt a measure of peace. But how would I navigate unknown medical and spiritual territory if my parents did not approve? Were they right? Was I missing something? Am I giving up? But I told Dan Snyder I would have the surgery. Would I go back on my word to the team's owner?

Was I prepared to walk this journey of recovery alone? What would that mean? This is the first time I began to feel a shift in who I was. Decisions I had made up to this point in my life were made with other people in mind, what they would think, how they would feel. I would worry about how things I chose to do would impact my family and friends. Now I began to ask: what is the best decision for me, for my body and my life? If this was the right question, why did it feel wrong to think this way?

I remember calling my parents and telling them of my decision: I would have knee surgery to repair the torn ACL. Growing up, one thing I could always rely on was the support of my parents. Whether it was getting through an injury in high school or deciding where I would attend college, I always felt their support. I felt they understood me and wanted what I wanted. This time was different. My parents did not want me to have the knee surgery. I was stunned.

I was almost twenty-five years old. I was in my fourth year in the NFL. I was the starting running back. But they are my parents. That makes everything different. When they did not support the plan for surgery, this was difficult, perhaps more difficult than the injury itself. Who I was and what I valued, how I thought, and what priorities I set, were guided by them. Suddenly I was making a life-changing decision without their support.

My parents were committed to instilling values of faith, respect for myself and others, and the ability to dream big. They are devout Christians. Their values guided me in high school, then in college, and in my first few years in the NFL. But a challenge began as I moved from being an adolescent to being an adult. As I was confronted with new kinds of challenges, I would recall lessons learned from my parents and factor their values as I faced new situations. Many times the way I looked at a situation and the decision I made were heavily influenced by the lessons they taught me. At other times, especially as I became an adult, there was a new influence. I felt an inner pull to go in a different direction.

I did not realize it at the time, but I was becoming my own individual, becoming separate from my parents. I was not rejecting them or their influence. But I was discovering that I had my own self, my own mind, my own soul. I was gaining confidence to make my own decisions and feeling good about them. Even before the need to decide about knee surgery, I had felt this inner pull. Still, I could not understand why my parents did not support the decision to have knee surgery. The owner had reassured me. Even before his call, I had begun to realize that surgery was the only way to repair a torn ACL.

As the Mayo Clinic website describes:

> *An ACL injury is a tear or sprain of the anterior cruciate ligament (ACL), one of the major ligaments in your knee. ACL injuries most commonly occur during sports that involve sudden stops or changes in direction, jumping and landing. Many people hear or feel a "pop" in the knee when an ACL injury occurs. Your knee may swell, feel unstable and become too painful to bear weight.*

Treatment may include rest and rehabilitation exercises to regain strength, or surgery to replace the torn ligament followed by rehabilitation. Surgery is required when the injury is severe or you are an athlete and need as much range of motion and power as possible, surgery is encouraged. During ACL surgery, the surgeon removes the damaged ligament and replaces it with a segment of tendon—tissue similar to a ligament that connects muscle to bone.

For my surgery, like the treatment of many other professional athletes, the tendon used came from the patella, or knee cap. For persons who are not professional athletes, the tendon often comes from the hamstring. But athletes use the hamstring to pivot and cut. To use it would limit my agility. So the patella tendon was used.

After surgery, Mayo explains, there will be a course of rehabilitative therapy. Successful ACL reconstruction paired with rigorous rehabilitation can usually restore stability and function to your knee. I knew that was coming and looked forward to it. It was the doorway to return to play, and I was ready, once the decision was made.

But the Mayo Clinic cautious that:

There's no set time frame for athletes to return to play. Up to one-third of athletes sustain another tear in the same or opposite knee within two years. In general, it takes as long as a year or more before athletes can safely return to play. Doctors and physical therapists will perform tests to gauge your knee's stability, strength, function and readiness to return to sports activities at various intervals. Strength, stability and movement patterns must be optimized before you return to an activity with a risk for ACL injury.

As the reality of the surgery and rehabilitation sank in, the issue with my parents became intense. I could not understand why my parents were so disappointed that I was not making the choice they felt I should make or even believe what they believed. Now having two sons of my own, I can understand their dilemma. As a parent, I now spend years trying to instill values into my children in hopes of forming their moral character and giving them the tools to succeed in life. But eventually, children make choices that challenge their parents' values. It seems incomprehensible. It can feel like rejection.

When I told my parents I had decided to have surgery on my left knee, it felt like I was giving up hope. Somehow, I was not the same kid who believed he was so strong he would never get sick. I was no longer the kid who called his doctor a liar when he said that I would not play football again in my senior year of high school. Three weeks later I rushed for over three hundred yards and scored five touchdowns in one game. The doctor attended that game and he was speechless. My parents proudly stood with me then. Now, when I am twenty-four years old, they disagree strongly.

Parental support was something I took for granted. Because I always had it, I never expected not to have it. Growing up, I knew kids who were more talented, who had more money and opportunities. But because their parents gave little support and had little involvement, these kids got caught up in the wrong crowd or lost the passion to develop their talents. I now see that a key to my success and resilience was the constant love and support of my parents.

Faith became a key factor. As I grew up, I naturally would pray first when I faced a tough decision. Sometimes prayer meant simply asking for what I thought I wanted or needed. I readily asked God to help me with school, with football, with family and friends. At other times, especially as I grew older, I would ask: God, who am I? Show me, God, what I am missing, teach me what I need to know. I was becoming more open, not just asking for things. As I became more open, I found I could be surprised. I would be led in a new direction. I would see possibilities I never imagined.

Prayer was often followed by writing. I would record my thoughts and emotions on paper. Taking the time to write made it real and helped me to concentrate on what was happening. Writing gave me an outlet. I could release my passions and organize my thoughts. Writing proved to be therapeutic. I would find myself starting to write out of anger, then feeling inspired by the time I had finished. I had worked through my frustrations and developed solutions. When writing wasn't enough, I would talk to my parents. But that was not the case with this knee surgery. Now I was doing it on my own.

Knowing what I know now, I still would have the surgery. In fact, I would have been more decisive and acted sooner. But I was learning something new and different. Like trying on new shoes, it felt stiff and uncomfortable. But it was the right decision, medically and spiritually. In his book Blink, Malcolm Gladwell says that "decisions made very quickly can be every bit as good as decisions made cautiously and deliberately." This was one of my first lessons in recovery. I was learning that recovery is not only a physical process, it is a psychological and spiritual process. I saw for the first time that recovery does not mean going back to the life I had before. Recovery means building a new and different life. Resilience takes you there.

It is a process. It entails learning to trust the voice within you. Some call it instinct. I believe it is a combination of your values plus your experiences plus your life's purpose. Like a baby learning to walk, I had to begin to walk this road on my own. Only I could take those first two steps and stand on my own feet in this new way. I had to accept what others were telling me. I had to learn from their experience. Then I had to apply what I heard to my life. I had to do it on my own.

At first, this seemed counterintuitive. Why would I accept something if I didn't believe it first? I was learning something about faith. It is not a set of beliefs or even an attitude. It is a willingness to step forward, to listen, and to heed what others share about their experiences. This was not easy. How do I know when someone is trying to help and not just forcing their reality on me? It seemed that the more information I received, and the more people asked and spoke up, the more difficult the situation became. How could I separate helpful information from mere opinion? In the past, there had been times when I was eager to prove people wrong. As a professional athlete, I had been trained to resist failure, to keep going until success was achieved. I tried to apply that here. But this was a new experience. My parents did not support the decision. I began to see that deciding whether or not to have the surgery was only the beginning. I was getting a crash course in decision-making and in faith.

Chapter Three

WHO WOULD HAVE IMAGINED?

The journey toward recovery became a journey through my life, back to the awakening of an intense motivation to succeed, especially in athletics.

I was a young kid who dreamed of a better life. My parents never worried about me getting into trouble. I wasn't interested in parties, drugs, or even girls. The one thing I wanted was to go pro. To do that I needed to excel in sports. I had to be the best in my school, my team, and my state. Only the best was acceptable.

I was never comfortable as a kid. I always wanted better. I remember numerous family holidays where everyone sat around eating and enjoying themselves. But I could not do that. Something didn't feel right. In my mind, I thought, "I could be getting better. I could be working on my game. This is where I can gain my edge." I would go for a jog, find the nearest field or track and run until I was exhausted.

I'm not sure when, but at some point, I took on a sense of responsibility for my family's success. My father was present. He worked and seemed to work hard. Yet for some reason, we were not able to make ends meet. Tensions between my parents grew as I became older. Even as a child I could sense times were hard and money was scarce.

With each family move and every argument about lack of financial resources, something was growing inside of me. At some point, I made up my mind that if things were going to change for my family, I would have to be the one to make it happen.

"Our deepest motivations develop slowly over time through the thousands of interactions we have with the important people in our lives. Our deepest motives consist of our attempt to live up to valued images of success—images of who we are and who we want to become.

"Our identities—our theories of ourselves—develop slowly in countless interactions with parents, teachers, mentors, friends, peers, and so forth."
(Michael Mascolo, PhD)

It seems ridiculous now that a sixth or seventh-grade child would feel responsible for his family's well-being. Some parents, and perhaps psychologists as well, would call this unhealthy. But I would argue with this opinion. I believe each child is driven by different factors. As a parent now, I realize that one of the most important things I must do is to help my children identify an inner passion. I loved the game of football. But it took on a deeper meaning for me. That inner drive to play for something and someone bigger than myself kept me focused. I'm not sure that I would have had the same drive, urgency, and focus had I not felt that way. That pressure never seemed overwhelming. It was life-giving.

Even as the drive percolated within me, I was becoming aware of so much. At times at Episcopal High School, in particular, I envied my teammates and their families. I watched parents pull up to games in the latest minivan or SUV. Life seemed to be good for them. I would hear them talk about where their family went for vacation, or their latest video gaming system and other luxuries. This motivated me. The playing field was my equalizer. No, I could not relate to the experiences they described, but I could outwork them. I could win. In my mind the more I dominated a game, the more I won, the less the socio-economic differences mattered. Football was an equalizer.

Now, parents often ask me to train their kids. This can be hard for me. It reminds me of the journey I took as a kid. Sports were everything to me. Yes, I enjoyed playing, but it was more than that. Getting that first down, or recovering that loose ball was a difference-maker. In my mind, it meant getting to the next level which would secure a better life for me and my family. Daily training was not an option—it was a necessity. It was part of who I was. Trying to explain that to a kid who does not know what it means to be hungry is tough. Sports wasn't one thing—it was everything. It was the doorway to a better life.

I recently had a conversation with a mom whose son was in a middle school football league. Most of the kids in this league came from middle to upper-class families. Their parents had jobs that paid well. Most of these kids did not have aspirations of playing at the highest level. Their idea of success was going to college, starting a business, and getting a good job with a steady 401k, then retiring.

This mom was reluctant to send her child to the other side of town to play against kids who only competed to win. Many of those kids viewed success differently than the suburban kids. Kids who grew up like me came from lower-income homes. Few of their parents had attended college. Unlike suburban parents, parents on the other side of town held minimum wage jobs. They had no retirement savings and did not own their homes. As much as they loved their families, their kids saw fewer future possibilities. These kids would have to create their own paths if they were to succeed. It would be a long journey. There would be little certainty for the kids from families with few economic means. These kids would have to prove themselves every day. They would need to be better.

This mom's fear was that her son may get hurt or not play based on the increased level of competition. As I listened to her, I reflected upon my days in little league sports. In a sense she was absolutely right: those "other" kids played to win. There was a deeper motivation and passion behind their efforts. I remember thinking as a kid, every time I stepped onto the field that no one wanted to be there as much as I did. Whether that was true or not didn't matter. That was my mindset. That was how I approached each game, even each play. I could see intimidation a mile away. Before games, I could hear it in my own teammates' conversations as they watched players from the opposing team walk up to the field or warm-up. Mentally they had already lost.

I always wanted to be a part of the best. I wanted to be challenged. This came from my parents. Both of my parents grew up in low-income housing and were determined to provide opportunities they had not had for their kids. They valued education. My mother always found the best schools for us to attend. But at school, there were not many kids who looked like me. The issue of race and the reality of difference was always in the background.

My family had moved to Tulsa, Oklahoma when I was in kindergarten. By then there were four kids. I have an older brother and sister and a younger sister. The move to Tulsa was part of our parents' journey, which had become a faith journey. Neither my father, who grew up on Long Island, nor my mother, who grew up in North Carolina, had faith backgrounds. They met in North Carolina when my father was in the Marine Corps, married, and then lived in California during my father's military service. When she became pregnant with her first child, my mother decided something needed to be different. She needed more in life. So, she became heavily involved in a church. A new, decisive chapter began for her.

In his own way, my father needed more. At first, he went to church simply because my mother went to church. He did not want her being hit on by other men. Then something clicked for him. Like her, he was searching for a foundation, for spiritual roots, for genuine belonging. But they needed guidance. The marriage was volatile. They argued a lot. One day, he actually started to leave. But he carried images of chaos, of havoc in the family, and he stopped. His own family had broken apart. He spent time in foster care until an aunt took him in. It would be challenging, but he would not repeat what he had gone through before. My parents had their personal frustrations and hurts from growing up. It was no surprise that they brought these to their marriage. But they worked at staying together. It became an important example for us as kids. By now, all four of us have graduated from college. Our parents did much that was right.

Early in my life, I became aware of the depth of faith my parents were cultivating. My mother, Nikkie Hightower, speaks eloquently about her faith and her approach to being a parent. "God is the center of all," she emphasizes. In turn, "children must be guided, channeled." Parents must provide structure. "Homework, activities, chores – everything has a place, everything must be regulated, including making decisions." My mother instilled an emphasis on purpose in my life. "Let your children know your course, your intention. Stay with it. Then nobody can take you off your course." She remembers that I was a very determined child. "Determined," she reflects now. "That is a good word. Tim was very decisive. He was in control of his emotions and his feelings, even as a child."

The move to Tulsa allowed my mother to attend Rhema Bible College and to take courses at Oral Roberts University. As kids, we often were left to play on the ORU campus while our mother studied. We lived just across the Arkansas River in Jenks, a suburb of Tulsa. Our father had hoped to study at Rhema as well. He and Mother had talked about becoming co-pastors of a church somewhere. But with our father working, only mother had the time to go further in her education. Looking back at it, my parents made a lot of sacrifices and never had much money. They wanted to get ahead, and they wanted their kids to get ahead.

For me that meant football. My father would remind me that he had quit his high school team. A new coach fired him as the team captain at the start of the season, so he walked off and never came back. That experience stuck with him. Did he expect me to go where he never went, to fulfill his own hopes that were never fulfilled? I have done much that he wanted to do. But he never pushed me. He would have supported almost anything I tried to do.

That did not mean I could get away with anything. Once, in the sixth grade, in the middle of the football, I became enraged at my teammates and showed it. I was out of control. My father charged onto the field and dragged me away. He pulled off my jersey and shoulder pads. Now he was enraged, and I was crying. He told me that if I did not have the right attitude, I would not play. It was a powerful lesson. The images remain vivid. Play the right way, he was teaching me. Show respect. Channel your passion. Keep your composure on the field. Be focused.

It was not all seriousness. He taught me to have fun. "Are you having fun? Do you love it?" My father wanted me to play football only if I loved it, enjoyed it, and knew how to handle it. That taught me something about teamwork, about respecting others, about playing hard and playing fair. You don't always appreciate lessons like that until later. But they became embedded in me. My parents gave me a framework, a work ethic. I began to realize what this meant: put your heart into it and the ball will follow, I heard a coach say. As my own faith grew, I knew this also meant that I must trust God in me. I am part of God and God is part of me, at all times, in the midst of all things. This thought has been a compass, pointing me in the right direction.

In Tulsa, football became a way of life. I attended the elementary and middle schools in Jenks. It is a community that is known for its successful high school football program. Since 1993, the Trojans have been a dominant force in the Oklahoma 6A high school football scene, winning sixteen championships between 1993 and 2015. The 1997 team, which went 14–0 and outscored its opponents 535–118, is considered one of the greatest high school football teams in Oklahoma sports history. In Oklahoma, I was one year away from attending nationally ranked Jenks High School. The Middle School was a place to groom for joining this successful program. Then, if I could do well at Jenks High School, opportunities at major colleges would appear.

Faith was becoming a major part of my commitment to football. Do good, get good. Do bad get bad. It was part of living my faith as I matured. I remember once I reached high school, during the week before each game I would write out my goals for that week. One-hundred seventy-five yards rushing, four touchdowns, seven catches, zero fumbles, win. I would then look up a Bible passage such as, "All things are possible to him who believes," and write it underneath the goal. Then I would write a daily confession or mantra, which I would read aloud every morning, before practice and prior to going to bed. I can do it.

I remember telling myself, over and over, that I would dedicate my thoughts and my actions this week and I would accomplish my goals. Many times, this worked. I would achieve or surpass my goal for the week. Other times it did not work out so well. Those times often left me confused. As a young child when I believed something, I believed it all the way. When I was told in church and by my parents that if I believed in something I could have it, that was that. I did not consider my age, perceived limitations or external factors that could prevent me from getting what I wanted. All I knew was what I wanted. I prayed and I would do whatever was necessary to make it happen.

This perspective was helpful. We live in a society driven by statistics. From the time we are born, society tells us how tall we will be, or how smart, how much income we can make, and so forth. As a young African American male, I am six times more likely to be incarcerated, more likely to be placed in special education classes (80 percent of special education classes are Black or Hispanic), more likely to earn less than my non-Black peers, less likely to own a home and more likely to get divorced. Hate it or love it these are the statistics. Even as a kid, you see them. You live them. From the schools you attend to the way people talk, this is the lens through which you could easily see things. Fortunately, my parents did not raise me to view myself this way.

But there are few straight lines in life. Before I reached high school in Jenks, Oklahoma, we moved again, this time to Prince George's County, Maryland. My siblings and I did not want to leave Tulsa, Oklahoma. Our friends were there and at the time, our hopes and future dreams were there as well. I remember my mom and dad telling us for the first time we were moving across the country to Maryland. What is a Maryland, I wondered, and why would we move there? Oklahoma seemed fine.

While I was aware of how much I stood out when I went to school, when I was home, things were OK. Kids in my neighborhood were more like me and we got along. None of us had or came from money and we knew it. Our conversations were not about where we went on vacation or the latest games and gadgets. Our conversations were about hope. Hope that our lives would be different one day. Our neighborhoods were filled with families of Black, Latino, and Asian descent. We all wanted to make it, to do better in life. We wanted to succeed, and to make our families proud. We knew that making it meant we had to be different. We had to be special, we had to stand out. None of us knew doctors, lawyers, or business people. They were not in our families. For that to change, it would have to start with us.

Sports were a common ground for me and my friends. It gave us something to hope for. As neighborhood kids, we would watch the NBA finals or NFL playoffs. The next day, we would gather and replay the scenarios with hopes that we would be the ones on tv someday. Most of my friendships were made through sports. Sports put us around people we would have never encountered otherwise. I would visit my white team-mate's houses. Big houses with pools, video games, and nice cars. They seemed to have it all. As a kid, I never understood why families in our neighborhoods had so little, while others seemed to have so much more. Was it hard work? Maybe. But that idea was a stretch for me. My parents both worked two and three jobs, yet we never seemed to have enough. Why weren't my parents doctors, lawyers, and CEOs? Were they not smart enough? The more I thought about it, all the doctors I went to were white. Maybe that profession was just not for us.

As my parents prepared for the move east, my brother and I were not happy. My mother wanted to make the move early in the summer so there was time to learn about the educational system in Maryland. Education was important to her. She made it her priority to give us the best education possible and to be involved. My father often tells the story of how my mother turned down a good job with the government to be a teacher. She wanted to understand the school system. Being a teacher ensured she would be home with us in the afternoon and during the summer. Hearing this story as a kid, I could not appreciate it. I thought, why would she turn down the money? We needed that money. Maybe we would not have struggled or moved around all the time. Maybe she would have been able to buy Christmas gifts on time and not on layaway.

As I got older, the sacrifice began to make sense. I noticed that my peers might have parents who made lots of money but who were rarely around or involved. On the surface, they had it all; yet they craved attention from their parents. As a result, they acted out and got into trouble. By contrast, my siblings and I knew we would have to answer to our mother for our decisions when we got home. There is no substitute for parental support and accountability.

My brother and I were still involved in summer sports in Oklahoma. We were in the middle of AAU basketball tournaments and wanted to finish our season. My parents decided we would put everything in storage and then drop my mother and sisters off in Maryland. My brother, father, and I would return to Oklahoma and finish off our summer tournaments. My brother and I knew this was big. A forty-hour round trip drive by our father so his kids could finish a commitment. More than sports, it was a lesson. It was always a lesson with my father. "Finish what you start." It would have been easy for my parents to prioritize their commitments over ours. We were kids. Adults' priorities take precedence. Greater than any words spoken, this decision by my parents showed us that our commitments matter. I will never forget that sacrifice. My brother and I practiced and played harder. We were grateful and wanted to show it.

At the end of the summer, we reluctantly packed our bags and said our goodbyes to friends with tears in our eyes. We arrived in Maryland a few days before school began. I would soon learn that I missed the sign-up deadline for fall football. I was in a new place and unable to play football. I hated Maryland already. On top of that, there was no school soccer team. "Black kids don't play soccer," I was told. I had no clue how I would make friends or fit in without football or soccer.

Chapter Four

TWISTS AND TURNS IN MARYLAND

Many things were different in Maryland. For the first time, I noticed the socio-economic gap as it pertained to academics.

Eugene Burroughs Middle School in Prince Georges County was where I began eighth grade. I was quiet and kept to myself. I was not the popular kid. According to my new classmates, I talked differently. I did not dress the same. I was not familiar with east coast swag: jean jackets, looney tunes gear, rubber bands on the bottom of the jeans to show off your new shoes. I did not really have a style. I was a California kid, who grew up in Oklahoma and now lived in Maryland. Zig-zag pants, surfer shorts and Dr. Maarten boots. I was a long way from a beach and my classmates let me know it. To hide my "country" accent, I kept quiet and spoke as little as possible.

Then there was the girl thing. Middle school was the time when everyone began to notice the opposite sex. Who was dating who was a big thing. I would watch classmates and teammates talk to girls with so much charisma and confidence. It seemed so effortless. I definitely noticed girls, I just did not know what to say. How do you approach someone you like? Do you walk up to her and say, "Hey, I like you"? No, that's too desperate. Maybe you send her a note. Do you like me? Check yes or no. Get her to commit first. I saw a few kids exchange notes under the desk in class or leave them in lockers.

But what if the wrong person found it? Too risky. Or maybe you play hard to get. That seemed like the cool thing. But how do I get her to pay attention to me in the first place? What do girls like? I have two sisters, maybe I could ask them? No, it's weird talking about girls to my sisters. We did not talk about sex or even relationships in my home. Too awkward I guess, or maybe it was against our religion. Ugh, why was this middle school thing so hard? It seemed easier to stay quiet and if a girl noticed me, she would say something. To girls, I quickly became known as the "shy guy." While this did not seem like a good thing then, as I wanted to be popular, it worked out well later in college.

I was not always shy. There was one time I did try. I remember watching a few guys tell their female friends about a girl they liked. The friend would relate the message and also put in a good word. Seemed like a win-win. Avoid potential embarrassment and boost my chances by having someone speak on my behalf. I went to Shevonne. She lived near my neighborhood. She was also an athlete. A basketball player. Most importantly, she was friends with Kemena, who was her teammate. Kemena was the girl who caught my eye. Shevonne, my best friend, Jabari, and I hung out in the neighborhood, played basketball, and talked about life. One day I went to Shevonne and told her about my crush on Kemena. "Will you let her know?" I asked. She agreed. I couldn't wait.

The next day in band class, Shevonne approached me. Her facial expression did not look good. I told Kemena, she said. OK, and what did she say? She said you are cute, but she did not like the way you dressed. She can't hang out with you if you keep wearing that jacket and those FILA shoes. I looked down at my shoes and at my jacket. The same ones I wore every day. In my family, my brother and I got two pairs of shoes a year. When we were younger, we wanted the same shoes, so that we could dress alike. As we got older, we used a bit more strategy. If we both got different shoes, we could have more of a selection to wear with four options as opposed to two. This worked until we both wanted to wear the same shoe on the same day!

So, I looked back up at Shevonne embarrassed. I had no clue what to do or say. Was this a yes? If so, it meant I had to change who I was to impress someone. Did she need to like me or my clothes? Something did not feel right. While I wanted the most popular clothes or shoes, I was OK with what I wore. Why did that matter to her? If she liked me, she liked me I thought. Suddenly Kemena began to seem less attractive. Embarrassed and halfway pissed off I shrugged my shoulders as if I did not care and said, oh well. I passed Kemena in the hallways many times that year. She never uttered a word. I guess she never liked me after all. Oh well, it was worth a shot. In the end, it felt better to be me instead of pretending to be someone I was not.

Middle school could not end soon enough. No football or soccer and no girls interested in me. I did play basketball, although our team was not very good. High school would be better I thought. But, when I arrived at Friendly High School, I felt more out of place than I had in middle school. I was already at the bottom of the food chain being a freshman. On top of that, my older siblings had established a reputation for being outsiders and I was their younger sibling. My older brother, Emmanuel, did his best to fit in. He changed his clothing style, quickly adopted the East Coast slang, and found a group of friends. My older sister, Qiana, rebelled. She was a junior and was upset about leaving her friends in Oklahoma in the middle of high school. On top of that, she refused to change the way she dressed, spoke, or acted. She had a hard time adjusting. Friendly belied its name. I never felt right in that school.

Then there was DeMatha High School in Hyattsville, Maryland. The first time I heard about DeMatha, I was drawn to it. DeMatha is an all-boys Catholic School. I saw excellence and I envisioned opportunity. I was serious about football: DeMatha has been a football powerhouse. I learned that they had top-of-the-line equipment and were well respected among college football coaches. To make it at DeMatha, you had to excel on and off the field. I embraced the challenge.

My father brought me to summer workouts at DeMatha, a few weeks prior to fall training camp. I quickly noticed I was not the best talent on the field and that was fine by me. I was ready to be challenged. I was ready to be in an environment that would prepare me for the next level I aspired to. Prior to the school year, DeMatha coaches informed my father the school was out of scholarships but they would do what they could to work with my family financially. It took some time getting used to an all-boys school. Not that I was dating anyone at the time, but I did miss seeing someone from the opposite sex from time to time. DeMatha was competitive. They had a freshman, junior varsity, and varsity team compared to JV and varsity at public school. To make varsity you had to be good. Really good. I was determined to make varsity as a sophomore.

In fact, I was the only sophomore to make varsity. This was big. This was the first true test of how I measured up against real competition. Top players from DeMatha often ended up playing Division I football and some even went on to play professionally. If I could make it here, I was well on my way, I thought. I did not play much, but this environment felt right. You know you are in a good place when the potential benefits outweigh the sacrifices. Waking up an hour earlier, arriving home an hour later, and not seeing much playing time did not affect me. I was in the right place for me.

My brother attended DeMatha but did not enjoy it the way I did. He wanted to stay at Friendly High School. He had built friendships and established his place on the basketball team. My brother resented my parents for this decision years later. My father was determined to keep us together. Every kid's needs are different. Parents must do their best to provide opportunities for their families while catering to the needs of each individual child.

DeMatha was located twenty minutes from Washington, DC. Often teammates would drive there after school or quickly during lunch for a change of scenery. I will never forget September 11, 2001. As I stared out of the window thinking about what I would eat for lunch and wondering if I would see the field for the next game, I remember my teacher receiving a phone call on the class phone. She seemed nervous. Immediately an alarm went off. The teacher rolled a television to the front of the room and turned on the news. Not understanding what was happening, we watched as a plane crashed into the World Trade Center. It did not seem real. What were we witnessing?

The teacher notified us that we were on lockdown and not permitted to leave. We continued to watch the news trying to wrap our minds around what was happening as we heard the news of another plane crashing into the Pentagon, less than twenty minutes from our school. We did not have cell phones to contact family and were instructed not to leave. For hours, we sat in the classroom glued to the television. I remember the uncertainty of everyone in the room. I quietly did what I often did in times of uncertainty. Closed my eyes and quietly said a prayer, "God keep us safe, bring us home safely," Amen.

A few weeks later there was another shock and this one was more personal. While I was in class, I was suddenly told to report to the front office. My father was waiting for my arrival. He did not seem happy. Apparently, coaches did not work things out financially and we were being asked to leave school. We could not afford tuition assistance let alone tuition. It was a full scholarship or else. My brother and I would have to leave DeMatha. Visibly upset, my father said a few choice words to the administration, and then we left. I remember feeling a bit embarrassed, but even more concerned. What would I do now? First Jenks, now DeMatha. What now? What will happen to my football aspirations? I wondered.

Back to Friendly High School we went, although this experience was not pleasant for my brother or me. Coaches and players resented us. We were the kids who thought they were too good for public school only to find out private school did not want us. I went from making DeMatha's varsity team to sitting on the bench on Friendly's JV team. Friendly did not have half the talent of DeMatha, yet the point was clear. Coaches valued loyalty and we were perceived as traitors. A common challenge in the Black community was where to send your kid to school. As a parent, you want better for your kid. Schools in inner cities were not properly funded and organized. I was fortunate to have a teacher present in class three-quarters of the time at Friendly. As black and brown families leave their communities in search of better academic opportunities, they leave neighborhoods, schools, and communities behind. Often kids and families are resented upon returning home.

This was the beginning of the tension between my brother and me. He too resented the school move. He blamed me. He felt my parents catered to my needs and he now had to forfeit his high school career because of it. So here I was, back at Friendly High school, playing JV football and tension building with my oldest brother.

A few weeks later, we received another phone call. My brother and I were asked to come to the principal's office. As we sat there, we learned that we were not in the proper school district and had been asked to de-enroll immediately. I remember my mom rushing through the door. I could see the steam coming from within her. Her motherly instincts kicked in as she raised her voice and challenged the principal. He shrugged his shoulders as if there was nothing he could do. At the time, half of the team lived out of the district, yet we were called out. The coaches never got over my brother and me leaving for DeMatha, and they made sure we paid for it.

In all, I attended three schools my sophomore year alone, including a brief stop at Westlake. Upon leaving DeMatha, my brother and I were out of school for almost a month. I still do not know how my mother managed to work two jobs, take us to and from schools, and handle such details as registrations and transcripts. I do not remember learning much and again I found myself without sports. Two out of my first three years in Maryland, I had missed sports. How would I make it to the next level, if I could not stay in one place long enough to play? How would scouts and prospective colleges find me? The instability affected me. My mother must have sensed this. She began to search for a solution.

Faith was a major part of this search. My perspective changed when we arrived in Maryland. The most important thing for my parents when we moved was to find a church home. The second was education. We began attending National Christian Church and then shortly after left and attended Spirit of Faith Christian Center under the leadership of Pastor Mike Freeman.

What drives an individual to dig deep within himself? To overcome obstacles? To ignore the limitations placed on him by others and society? For me, it started at home. Struggle was common growing up. The older I got the more I knew that life was hard for us. What stood out was how my father responded to difficult times. I remember overhearing conversations that we were being evicted and had less than forty-eight hours to leave. My dad always seemed positive. He always believed he would find a way. I couldn't understand how we could struggle so much and seem to have so little. Yet he spoke as if he would conquer the world and have everything he ever dreamed of at his fingertips. Was he delusional? He was a boxer. At times I worried he had taken too many hits during his career and was losing his mind. My dad would make comments as we were approaching a crowded parking lot like "my parking spot will be waiting on me when I get there." Or "I always get the best parking spots." Sometimes it worked out, often it did not.

Regardless of the outcome he was convinced that his words and what he believed had power; that his belief was more important than any external force or outcome. He would watch games on television. Even if the game was a blowout with no chance for a comeback, he loved to cheer for the underdog.

He would emotionally get into the game while saying, "it's not over, there is still time on the clock." The thing that tripped me out was when the game was over, he would be upset when the team he was cheering for lost. As if he expected them to win after being down by thirty points with three minutes left. I often wondered, what world does he live in?

My dad did not believe in being realistic. "What is realistic? Who told you to be realistic?" He hated it when I came home and told him what a teacher or coach told me was possible. "Who told you that?" He would ask angrily. "I didn't tell you that. Never be defined by the limitations of man. With God, all things are possible, son." I did not understand it at the time, but I needed this passion. I needed this mindset.

As I got older, I adopted this mindset. I found myself responding to my peers with strong convictions. Whenever someone told me what I couldn't do or have, I challenged them just as my father did. "I can do anything." "Why can't I?" became regular parts of my vocabulary. Looking back, I had no idea what I was doing. If you repeat something enough, whether right or wrong, you will soon believe it. It did not matter what I didn't have. I could do it. I could have it.

Recently I had a conversation with my college roommate. We talked about the state of young men in society. We talked about fatherlessness and the effect it had. It amazed me to see statistics of incarceration, mental illness and suicide were all being led by fatherless men. As a young kid, I looked to my father for identity. I reflected on his attitude, mindset, and demeanor. I took on challenges as I watched him take on challenges. I prayed as he prayed in tough times. No matter how tall the task, I believed the best because that's what my father did. Not that he was perfect, but he was there. As an adult, I've formed my own beliefs and no longer approach every challenge the way my father did. Yet there are times I still refer to my dad. When I question my strength or capability to handle a situation, to lead my family, I draw strength from thinking of my dad. I reflect back on the childhood stories, obstacles we faced, and words he planted inside me. What happens when you do not have a father, or you have one who is not present for you?

This is a widespread challenge. Before I developed my own confidence, I relied on my father's confidence in me. Young and old men are facing insurmountable challenges without a clear identity. Who was in their lives when they were young, telling them they will make it, showing them how to persevere? This is not to take away from our mothers; they carried burdens for far too long. There are many children who grow up without fathers and yet are mentally and emotionally strong just as there are many who grow up with fathers but are not secure.

Ask any kid who did not grow up with a father or a positive representation of a man. Find a father you respect. If you can talk to him, ask him to help you. Ask him to teach you. Perseverance is taught and learned. If you do not have someone you can ask, study someone. The books on fatherhood by Lebron James and Bishop T.D. Jakes are examples. Learn from those whom you admire, people who have proven themselves in this area. The more you hear their words and stories you will soon find yourself talking as they talk and acting as they act.

Seventy-seven percent of Americans say that religion is at least somewhat important in their lives, and 83 percent say they're fairly certain that God or a higher power exists[1].

1   David B. Feldman PhD. "Is Religion Good or Bad For Us?" Psychology Today. Sussex Publishers LLC, 10 Sept 2018, accessed 18 February 2022, https://www.psychologytoday.com/us/blog/supersurvivors/201809/is-religion-good-or-bad-us

In search of educational opportunity, my mother took me on a few school visits, including private schools. When we arrived at the open house for Episcopal High School, I remember watching the video. I had no idea what a boarding school was. Why would a parent send their kid away in high school? These kids must be bad. Is this a military school? Everyone seemed to be smiling in the videos. It seemed staged. Just tell me straight. But my younger sister Victoria loved it. She and I were close. I remember that she wanted to go. That was enough for me. If she was going, I was going. I would not let her go alone. I wanted to look out for her. Plus, it seemed better than where I had been, so it was worth a shot.

Chapter Five

ENTERING A NEW WORLD

There was a basic reason why the private school world became a reality. It was more than what my parents wanted: I wanted better. That meant, first, figuring out what "better" meant and then deciding how to live into it. Obviously, "better" meant academic as well as athletic challenge. Living into being "better" took me into a world I had never seen.

DeMatha had given me a taste of the challenge I craved. It was a competitive environment academically and athletically. While I was aware of the lack of girls around me in this all-male school, it did not bother me. On the other hand, Episcopal was a shock for which I was not prepared. That shock had nothing to do with girls on campus.

In the summer of 2001, prior to my junior year in high school, my mother was determined to find a better academic opportunity for me and my younger sister. My older sister, Qiana, had just graduated, and my older brother, Emmanuel, made it clear that he had no intention of leaving public school. He was smarting from the decision to remove him from Friendly High School against his wishes.

I remember attending open houses for prep schools in the vicinity of Washington, D.C. At each open house, school representatives droned on about why they were the best and what they had to offer students and their families. I remember thinking: How do I know who is telling the truth? How do I determine which school is right for me? I recalled my experiences at DeMatha, Friendly, and Westlake. What did I like and not like about these schools? Criteria became clear. First, the school had to be competitive athletically. Sports had already taught me that in order to be the best you have to beat the best. Moving around a lot as a kid had its advantages. I was always the new kid on the block with something to prove. It is important to be challenged in this way early in life.

Competition made me better. It elevated my game. I did not have to be the best initially, I just had to hang around long enough to rise to the occasion. I remember my pastor talking about the importance of being in the right environment for personal growth. He would say "Some plants need more sun, more water and others less." My growth required entering competitive environments. It frustrates me to see young kids talk about the challenge of adjusting to college where "all of the kids are smart" or everyone is bigger, stronger, and faster. I wonder if they are used to being challenged.

Second, the next school could not be too far from home. DeMatha was almost an hour commute each way. Byron Westbrook, the younger brother of running back Brian Westbrook, lived nearby. He would drive me and another teammate to school each morning and take us home after practice. We spent hours each week in a car telling jokes, talking sports, and listen-

ing to music. I recall times when the car swerved as we struggled to wake up in the early mornings or fought exhaustion after
a long day of school and practice. I loved the school, but the
drive wore on me.

Finally, mentorship and coaching mattered a great deal. I
heard Michael Jordan talk about the influence of coach Dean
Smith while at North Carolina or seeing players impacted by
Georgetown coach John Thompson. Great players had great
coaches and mentors at some point in their lives. I also heard
talented young men talk about how the lack of support and guidance negatively affected them. My father often recalls the time
when he quit football. He had been determined to make the most
of his athletic ability. Despite his family being pulled apart, he
worked for the chance to play sports at the collegiate level. But
there was what he describes as a racist encounter with a newly
appointed coach, who fired him from being team captain heading into his senior season. "I was so upset I quit. I walked away
from it all. I did not have the guidance. I did not know how to
deal with it." Hearing the pain of regret and a missed opportunity stuck with me. I knew it would take the right guidance for
me to reach my full potential. The next school had to be a place
where I could learn and grow.

I did not want to be in a large place where I could feel lost.
I wanted my teachers and coaches to know who I was so their
help would be readily available. While I never admitted it, I
needed attention. Overcrowded public schools were not for me.
I did not have easy access to teachers who spent most of their
time trying to get disruptive students to pay attention. There
was not enough time to stimulate curiosity and the desire to
learn among engaged students. To be fair, those students acting

out needed the attention as well. They had their challenges, as did I.

I liked Bullis High School in Potomac Maryland. However, Bullis would not accept my sister Victoria so that was a no-go. We were a package deal. If a school wanted me, she had to go and vice versa. My parents worked long days and could not have three kids in three different schools. My dad was determined for us to stick together as a family, not be separated as his family was when he was young. Still, after a few visits to schools, I was exhausted and ready to move beyond the experience. Maybe this was just not for me.

Then we received an invitation to an open house for Episcopal High School, in Alexandria, Virginia. The event was not at the school. Instead, it was at the home of a current student. On top of that, the family was African American. I was surprised but willing to go. The open house was in Fort Washington, Maryland, not far from where my family lived. Victoria and I went.

When we arrived, the environment immediately was familiar. There were other kids and families from my background. I could smell the home-cooked meal when I walked in the door. With the other private schools, it was all about them, their program. I met them on their turf. They said all the right things but had not thought about my experience or what would make my sister and me feel welcome. Mr. and Mrs. Jones were the host family of the Episcopal High School open house. Being in their home and sensing the meal being prepared put me at ease.

Few things have the ability to impact mood and memory like the smell, taste, and even thought of food. As I walked through the door, the smell of warm apple pie, fresh-baked cornbread, yams, and collard greens elicited a sense of safety and security. The smell alone re-created a familiar environment of Sunday meals after church and holiday family gatherings. As a kid, I looked forward to this smell. It represented family, connection. Our family times were rare. My parents were from New York and North Carolina. Grandparents and extended family did not live nearby. When we gathered, important questions could be answered, usually over food. What were my parents like as kids? What did my grandparents experience when they were young? Where does my last name come from? It was all about identity.

As I surveyed the room full of black and brown families gathering to hear about Episcopal High School, I realized we were there for the same reason: better opportunity. The familiar smells of food were reassuring. But a new question soon arose. Of all my school visits, this was the first time I began to think about what my family and these families had in common. We all knew the feeling of loving our communities but facing the hard reality: we had to leave in order to search for better opportunities. It was more than Episcopal requiring students to board. It was facing the prospect of leaving the sense of community that had nurtured us.

How could we make things better if we abandoned our communities? Is this the decision black and brown families who came before me faced when integration began? Many students had promised to "come back" after they made it, but few did. Am I about to perpetuate this cycle? I struggled with this thought, even as I plunged into the meal. Fried chicken, collard greens, green beans, two rolls, one big scoop of macaroni and cheese, a side of stuffing (the corner piece of course), and at last the potato salad. Soul food turned an open house into a family gathering. It created an unspoken connection, which joined generations and linked us closely.

For decades, Southern Blacks had found ways to leave, to go North, in search of opportunity. The end of slavery brought sharecropping, discrimination, persecution, and limited opportunities. The Great Migration northward happened in waves of people, who worked to recreate home and to preserve the culture and family life they had built. Food was a critical factor. African enslaved people had to feed their families with less desirable ingredients, yet they took those scraps and turned them into a cultural cuisine. Slaves were forced to eat the animal parts their masters threw away. They cleaned and cooked pig intestines and called them "chitterlings." They took the butts of oxen and christened them "ox tails." Same thing for pigs' tails, pigs' feet, chicken necks, smoked neck bones, hog jowls, and gizzards. Soul food represents strength, identity, community. This was the connection and the identity I craved. As I sat at the table and listened to stories, I recognized that while parts of my own journey were unique, the struggles, challenges, and motivations I faced were more common than I had realized. A new awareness was born even as I entered a new world.

Bridget Johnson spoke on behalf of Episcopal admissions. She was a young track athlete who understood the needs of prospective students and their families. The video she showed did not resonate with me. It actually turned me off. I wondered how I could fit in there. I did not come from money. I did not dress, look or act like those kids. How would I connect with the faculty? The class size was ideal, but would they understand me? Also, athletics did not seem to be a priority. Almost as bad, the school was entirely for boarding students. I would have to live there. I could not go home during the week.

As my interest wavered, I glanced at my sister, Victoria. She seemed to love it. She was sold. The pros and cons became clear. The images in the video were not appealing. But I thought about the Jones family. I thought about Bridget Johnson. Since she was the track coach, maybe I could work with her to get faster for football. Ultimately, the open house and my sister sealed the deal. I would attend Episcopal High School for the next two years.

My mother, Nikkie Hightower, recalls that open house as a turning point for me and for my younger sister. "We saw opportunity in the open house. We also saw the school was serious about diversity. The food and the fellowship made it an easy decision. The people at Episcopal saw Tim and Victoria's maturity. It was a very proud moment for our family. I thought of all the prayers that had gone up before God. We knew we would keep going on this journey."

I could not wait to get started there. I had two years to secure a college scholarship. It felt good to have the uncertainty behind me. Now there could be fresh focus. I arrived at preseason football in shape and ready to go. The competition was different from DeMatha. The talent was not the same nor was the drive. It was not that these kids did not like football; it was that they did not need football. I needed it and was used to playing with kids who needed it. My scholarship and future NFL aspirations depended on it. I did not place much emphasis on meeting new friends and socializing. I was here for business. Looking back, it seems that my EHS teammates could not understand my focus. I certainly did not understand theirs. If I dropped a ball or made a mistake, I was angry. I obsessed about it until I could get it right. It bothered me when others laughed when they made a mistake. They did not seem very serious.

In the classroom, the first semester of school was a struggle. Episcopal High School is a college preparatory school. The class schedule and workload are designed to prepare students for managing time between academics and extracurricular activities. Some days I would have three classes; other days I would have two. During the off periods, I was expected to use my time to study. This was a big adjustment. It felt overwhelming. I was not a big reader then and reading was something we did every day. Lots of it. I did not know how I was to do homework and read seventy-five to 100 pages each day. On top of that, there always seemed to be a paper to write. Three- to five-page papers were a norm. At public school, papers were something you wrote at the end of the semester. You had time to prepare and write them. I was not used to this level of time management, reading comprehension, and writing. My grades showed my lack of readiness.

Yet the small community of students and faculty proved beneficial for me. Rather than let me fall behind, teachers reached out to see how they could help. I did lose all free periods and was placed in study hall. I knew I had academic support and I was willing to do the work, I just needed help. I did not know how to study. Looking back, I ask myself, why did I not just ask for help? Fortunately, I was in a small school that provided the attention and was proactive.

When I thought back to the open house, it hit me. I thought about the track coach and admission director Bridget Johnson. I thought about my concerns of having teachers who understood me. I was used to having my parents, church group, and adults who looked like me nearby. There were only a handful of African American students at EHS and none were my teachers.

Once I spoke with Ms. Johnson, I felt better. The connection to her would be a key to my success at the school and beyond.

Bridget Johnson echoes my experiences and thoughts. Especially for students of color and their families, the Episcopal High School experience became very personal. She recalls open houses for prospective students vividly. She wanted people to know they would be supported. She and others would be there for them. Being an athlete herself helped. When my foot was broken at Episcopal, she helped me to train and to recover. We would stay in touch and she would be a continuing resource. My parents also were supportive. "Because we lived nearby," my mother recalls, "we visited Tim at Episcopal often. We went to every football game and also came over sometimes for dinner."

To my surprise, I did not experience racial issues with classmates or teammates initially, though it became clear there was a divide. I remember a few conversations with female classmates. I was the new guy on campus, so naturally, there was curiosity and interest from the opposite sex. The problem was that I was Black and not from the legacy pedigree. Legacy meant that none of my family or previous generations attended Episcopal or any school like it. On one occasion a girl told me she liked me but could never date me because her friends and family would never accept me. While she would not call them racist, I understood. So, I kept to myself in this different world. I saw classmates leave for the weekends in limos or hang confederate flags outside of their dorm rooms. It bothered me but what could I say? I did not talk to them and they did not talk to me. There were a handful of ethnic kids and we quickly got to know each other. We ate together and hung out on the weekends. It was unspoken. We stuck together.

My grades gradually picked up as I began to excel on the field. There were tutors who helped with the classroom transition from public school. On the field, we were mediocre as a team, which I did not like, but I did like the attention. I liked the pressure of my teammates and coaches relying on me each game. Regardless of the socioeconomic or racial differences, when we stepped on the field, it was my time to shine. The focus was on success.

Yet success takes time. In high school, I wanted to be recognized as a top athlete. I worked hard, convinced that good things should happen for me. What I did not realize was how hard others also worked to realize their dreams. The summer before entering Episcopal, I had gone to a regional event at Temple University in Philadelphia. There were hundreds, maybe thousands, of rising juniors and seniors, all with collegiate and many with NFL aspirations. We were tested on how fast we ran, how high we jumped and how strong we were. At the time I did not lift weights. But my father had emphasized being in control of body and mind. That meant doing pushups, running hills, jumping rope, and stretching were the basis of my exercise regimen. I was not as developed physically as a lot of the kids who came to Temple and it showed.

They asked us to perform a bench press exercise. We were to press 185 pounds as many times as we could. It did not seem like a lot. I weighed close to 190 pounds at the time. I watched as each athlete took his turn, studying their technique because I had never done this before. When my name was called, I sat down just as I had seen the prior kids do. Eight reps I heard the coach say. Was that a lot? I stood around to watch others, this time to count the repetitions. A kid who stepped up weighed perhaps 145 to 150 pounds. I watched him perform fifteen reps.

How could that be? This kid was noticeably smaller than me yet stronger. How could that be?

The rest of the event became a blur. All I could think about was being outperformed by someone who was smaller. Then determination kicked in. This could never happen again. There had been a new realization, an awakening. The world became bigger than my neighborhood, city, and even state. As hard as I thought I worked, there were kids all over working just as hard and even harder. It challenged me to push myself. Over the next two years, I kept that experience in mind. I began lifting weights, running track, and reading books to learn how to be bigger, stronger, and faster.

During my senior year at Episcopal, as I would hear my peers naming scholarship offers they received, I tried to pretend that I was supportive. But deep down it was hard for me to wrap my mind around the fact that I had not received a single scholarship offer. Not one. I tried to reason with myself. Maybe I got lost in the shuffle. I did attend four high schools, three my sophomore year alone. Coaches were probably looking for me and just did not know where I was. None of the rationale helped. The bottom line was I did not have a college scholarship to show for the hard work invested. The idea that I wasn't good enough never crossed my mind. Even when I got to the NFL. My first season, I did many interviews where I was asked how college coaches had missed me. How did they not see the talent? This was music to my ears. It was proof that so many college coaches got it wrong. Something was wrong with them, not me.

Life's hardest challenge is to look yourself in the mirror, be honest and say I'm not good enough yet. Yet is the key word. It's a fine line because I was taught to have confidence in myself, to believe anything is possible. But, to get where I wanted to be,

I needed to admit where I was. "Yet" allowed me to ask what I must do to get there. I look back at the work I did after the Philadelphia experience prior to entering Episcopal. I reflect over the four years of two and often three-a-day workouts in college. Six years of grueling, humbling work. Honestly, I was not ready. I did not know the preparation it took to succeed at the next level. I needed to be exposed, to fail, and, above all, to understand failure and move ahead. That realization drove me daily.

Episcopal High School was a new world, on and off the football field. Tradition was big at EHS. Woodberry Forest was our rival, one of the longest-standing prep rivalries in the South. From the first day I stepped onto campus, the theme among teammates, coaches, and fellow classmates was "beat Woodberry." I did not care about Woodberry. I was not a legacy kid. I had no prior connection to the school. I soon grasped the importance. It was more than a game. Alumni traveled from around the world to attend the "big game." For me, it is necessary to win regardless of our opponent. Woodberry was just another team on the schedule. Even if it was the last game of the season, who cares about winning that game if you lose the first eight or nine?

That year we beat Woodberry 35–7. One of the largest margins in school history. Students rushed the field. I sat in the locker room with a blank face as everyone celebrated. All I could think about was the three or four games we lost by less than a touchdown. Where was this energy then? If we could have played in those games with half the intensity we mustered for the Woodberry game, we could have won those other games easily. I struggled with how to make sense of it. In my senior year, however, we lost. I struggled to understand in a different way. As I walked off the field that day, I felt that I had let my school down and I would never get another chance to make it right. It frustrates me to this day. I wanted to win every game we played.

Still, life at EHS was a turning point in several respects. I was not only creating my own space, I began to learn to be a "team player." It was hard. It would take time. I wanted to win and was willing to do whatever it took. Winning was how I defined success. To realize my goal, I had to win. I had a low tolerance for people who did not care about winning. As a result, I collided with coaches, players, and teachers on campus. My mind drifted in class as I daydreamed about football practice. I would practice my signature on my desk and at times leave it on the whiteboard before leaving class with a message underneath: "This will be worth a lot of money one day."

I just did not get it, the teachers and other students must have thought. This is an academic institution. School came first. They tried to instill "life lessons" and values. I was not interested. Your values do not work where I am from, I thought. The only thing that mattered was success. You succeed or you struggle. None of them had been evicted or worried about finding their next meal. How could they teach me about life? I started to lose respect for my coaches. I wanted the standard to be higher. They were too nice, I felt. I decided to create my own standard. It is hard to play a team sport alone. There was more to learn about teamwork.

Chapter Six

DON'T TELL ME WHAT I CAN'T DO

"Not caring what others think is likely to be the best choice you will ever make." By the time I entered the University of Richmond that message had become embedded in my mind. Various people in my life had sent this message, especially my father. He could become very angry if I told him what a coach or teacher said about me. "What other people think is not your business," he would respond. His words were magnified by the pain and regret I saw on his face and in his life. Not rarely, but constantly. I resolved that I could not let other people dictate who I am and how I feel about myself. No one would tell me what I can't do.

There was nothing casual or partial about my conviction. The chance to move beyond Episcopal High School and into college football was not just an opportunity. It was THE opportunity. I had to make it. I had to prove what I could do, beyond others, regardless of how good or how determined they might be. I would make it. There was no other option. I had nothing else and no one else on whom to rely. College football players would be faster, smarter, and more talented than in high school. They would also be more motivated. Football for them would be a priority, the way it was for me. More than ever, I had to prove myself.

That intensity had blossomed at Episcopal High School. Nothing would stop me. In my senior year at Episcopal, I had broken my foot. Doctor after doctor told me I couldn't play. That was unacceptable. Since the fourth grade, I had invested my life in playing football. No one was going to tell me I couldn't play. Finally, one doctor said I could play, and he would treat me if I wore a walking boot seven days a week, except when I was on the field. I agreed. I worked out in the swimming pool early in the morning five days a week with a track coach as well as working out with the football team. I finished the season rushing for nearly a thousand yards despite being able to play in only a few games. I would not be stopped.

But word of my broken foot, constantly in a boot, spread among college coaches. Before the injury, coaches from various colleges had contacted the athletic office at Episcopal. After the injury, the phone stopped ringing. It must have appeared that I was damaged goods. But the University of Richmond kept calling. Head Coach Jim Reid and one of his assistants, Jeff Hanson, kept visiting, encouraging, selling their school. At first, it seemed they were wasting their time. I had never heard of Richmond, other than it was a small school.

I looked into it and went for a visit. It seemed unlikely, a small university of less than 4,000 students set in an upscale suburb of Richmond, Virginia, a historically conservative city. But the university and the city clearly were growing, expanding, becoming more diverse. In the 1980s, the University of

Richmond Spider basketball team began making a national impact, and the football team was not far behind. In the early 2000s, the football team began going to the Division I playoffs regularly. The feeling grew that the school was building something I could help to extend.

Richmond has not produced many players who have gone on to the National Football League, but there have been some. That gave me hope. I knew I could make it. I knew I would make the most of this opportunity. I was more determined than ever. Determination to succeed on the football field was my defining trait. It overshadowed everything else in my life. Nobody was going to tell me what I could not do.

To my surprise, after a visit, I realized that Richmond was a fit. They wanted me, and I had begun to want them. When I analyzed it, the situation became clear. Even with the broken foot, coaches Reid and Hanson saw something in me. They saw potential. I even began to feel celebrated. In a smaller school that was building athletic as well as academic success, I would not feel lost. It was my only scholarship offer, but I leaped at it. Richmond would be the next step in developing my football ability.

Even so, there were times when things happened that I could not control. Just when things seemed settled, two weeks after I signed to attend the University of Richmond on a football scholarship, I learned from friends that Coach Reid was leaving to go to Syracuse. None of the Richmond coaches called me; I had to hear it from friends. The new coach, Dave Clawson, had his own approach and priorities, as I would soon learn. By my sophomore year, it was clear that he would focus on players he had recruited, players who seemingly matched his approach. Given this reality, I was more determined than ever to prove myself. I would succeed, regardless.

I will never forget my arrival at the University of Richmond. I was impatient to get there and increasingly impatient with my parents who drove me down from Maryland. As we neared the campus they began arguing. I was beside myself. Couldn't they share my excitement for once, just for a few minutes? More than ever, I was determined to succeed on my own terms, not on anyone else's.

When I finally was alone in my new dorm room, I began decorating my side, posting pictures and inspiring slogans on the wall. I even posted motivational sayings on the ceiling so I could study them while lying in bed. I began to devote every moment to the pursuit of excellence, to improve myself in every identifiable way. I even prayed that first night on campus. I told God that I wanted to leave a mark, to have a sense of purpose that would be admired and remembered. I would do all I could. I would get the most out of this opportunity.

Determination had to become action. Every aspect of my performance had to improve. A key detail was the forty-yard dash which measures a running back's speed. When I arrived at Richmond, I was timed at 4.9 seconds in the forty-yard dash. But to make professional football, I would have to be faster. I resolved that my speed would improve to 4.3 and to do whatever was needed to reach that goal. I wrote that this was the goal on a sheet of paper and left that paper on a coach's desk. I wanted my dedication made plain.

The coaches did not think it was possible. Some of my teammates shared the doubt. A few, seeing my intensity, even needled me. I doubled down. I had declared what I would do and I would do it. End of discussion. No other possibilities were allowed.

To reach the goal of a faster forty-yard dash, I joined the track team and ran sprints. The outcome was not stellar. In every meet, I finished last. But I had dedicated myself. I had decided that more speed was crucial. I would make it work.

Only once did I not finish last. It was in a track meet at Morgan State in Baltimore, where my brother, Emmanuel, was a student. I ran a race then went off with Emmanuel to grab a bite to eat. I assumed I was last. Someone had to find me to bring me back to the track. Somehow, I had qualified for the next race. It never happened again. In any case, I finished next to last.

Nevertheless, slowly, my determination to run faster paid off. I never stopped working. In my junior year at Richmond, I ran the forty-yard dash in 4.6 seconds, and in my senior year, I reached 4.4 seconds. Coaches and teammates were surprised. But I wasn't. I did not exult, I simply reminded myself that I had committed to the goal of 4.3, and I almost reached it.

I also doubled down on emulating great football running backs. I read somewhere that Emmitt Smith, the star running back, had taken ballet in college. Smith spent fifteen years in the NFL, primarily with the Dallas Cowboys, and went to three Super Bowls. He loomed large in my imagination. Ballet apparently had improved his agility. So, seeking every path to improvement, I took a class in ballet in Richmond. It's not clear what I gained. But it illustrated my focus, maybe even preoccupation.

I studied all of the great running backs, trying to understand what had made them great. I could not share their physical attributes. Yet I could learn from their techniques, their preparation, their forms of dedication. As I did, I reached a turning point in life. It crept up on me, and I did not fully grasp it at the time. It would surface again and again. The issue was the extent to which I could be coached, beyond my own intensely focused desire.

It was a long-standing issue. At the church my family attended when I was a child, there was a man who tried to give me advice about my life. It sounds presumptuous but, looking back, it is clear that he meant well. I listened to him for reasons I would only understand later. But when he spoke, in my mind, I pushed back. It sounded like he wanted me to live up to external standards set by other people. It couldn't possibly be about me. He touched a very sensitive emotional spot.

Even as a child, I was powerfully driven internally. Looking back, that drive was profoundly spiritual. It was a drive to find myself, to realize my true identity, to find lasting meaning. I was determined to prove myself on my own terms, which may have been the stumbling block. But I needed to assert myself, as we all do. I had to find worth within, though I would be compelled to face realities outside myself that challenged me.

Football had become the means, the center of my pursuit of self-realization. Each of us faces a path, a means toward the very goal for which I reached. External measures always come into play. That's what we need of each other, that's how we assess each other. Thus, I had to run a faster forty-yard dash, as a measure of my success. But it was my emerging internal self that fueled this drive to succeed. In my life, as in anyone's life, the external and the internal must align. My path to that alignment was sheer focus on football, with the conviction that no one could tell me what I could not do.

It could not all arise internally, within me. It could not simply be about increasing speed. I was learning that I was accountable. I was part of a team, representing a university, answering to the coaches. That did not always go well, despite my obvious determination. The coaches advised me to play to my strengths, as they saw them. Thus, at Richmond, the challenge was to develop my football skills and to develop my ability to work with others who could teach me things, even if I was not always ready to hear them. My vision of what this meant, and the vision of the coaches, clashed. This was especially the case with Richmond's head coach during my time there, Dave Clawson.

I was number three on the running back depth chart in 2005, my sophomore year. The player ahead of me, who was a freshman, had been recruited by Coach Clawson. Then, midway through the season, neither of the other running backs could play. In our next game, against James Madison, I rushed for 119 yards and scored two touchdowns while carrying the ball twenty times. I gained nearly six yards each time I ran. Finally, I had gotten the break I needed. I would not look back.

In the remaining four games of the regular season, we won handily, and I rushed for more than one hundred yards in each game. Against our traditional rival, William & Mary, I gained 111 yards on twenty carries and we won 41–7. We had lost three of our first four games, beating only Maine by five points. Then we rallied, turned the season around, and I was a prominent part of our recovery. It felt good. It felt even better that we had advanced to the Division I playoffs and were matched against Furman, ranked number three in the country in our division.

Then the bottom almost fell out. I overslept one morning and missed a final examination in one of my classes. I was on the path to resolving the matter. Then I was summoned to see the football coaching staff. Clawson, the head coach, assailed me verbally. He was frustrated and he was critical. I fumed, then steaming, clenching my fists.

Seeing my response moving in a bad direction, an assistant coach, Latrell Scott, also African American, grabbed me. He forced me out of the office, through the hall, and into a vacant room. Scott got in my face in a different way. He told me to cool off, to think about the incredible opportunity I would ruin if I did something foolish. He pledged to handle the situation if I would back off. I did. The academic aspect was handled, and I remained on the team. But things were not resolved.

Coach Clawson would make his point about his authority and my role as one of his players. In the Furman game, he kept me on the bench for the first half. When I entered the game in the third quarter, I was on fire. I carried the ball fifteen times for ninety yards. With one minute left in the game, and losing by four points, we were near the Furman goal line. It was fourth down, and I insisted on being given the ball. I knew I could score the go-ahead touchdown. But an attempted pass by our quarterback was incomplete and we turned the ball over to Furman. We lost, 20–24, on that December afternoon.

This loss sticks with me to this day. It was one of the first introductions to the consequences of my actions and how my decisions affect others. Who cares how talented you are if you are not reliable? When my team needed me the most, I sat on the sidelines because of a selfish decision. I could either blame my coach or take responsibility. It was an important lesson about balancing the good of the team with my own sense of what I needed.

However, the 2005 season was a turning point. I had begun to show what I could do. My determination deepened even as my relationship with the coaches, especially Clawson, remained tense. Looking back, Latrell Scott's timely intervention was telling. I would realize later that an African-American coach would have special sensitivity. He would recognize a dynamic that a white coach might easily miss.

All coaches want to recruit and play kids who are hungry to compete and to win. For many African-American kids, it's more than a game. Sports becomes everything, the only obvious road to success in life. They may have grown up in broken families, in strained economic situations, and in troubled neighborhoods. Arriving at a notable college on scholarship, being presented with resources that they've never seen, the opportunity to be there becomes incredibly rare. Yet these kids can be vulnerable, more so than other young adults. One reason for their vulnerability is that their coaches and others in authority become larger than life.

I was fortunate to have devoted parents and, especially, a strong father. But, as they develop, kids always need other authority figures. Kids from single-parent situations and broken homes are especially in need, whether they are aware of this need or not. For some student-athletes, coaches can become like fathers. It is easy to be devoted to one's coaches. They guard the gateway to athletic success. But they can be more.

It is also easy to become disenchanted with one's coaches. They loom incredibly large. The intense pursuit of success fosters a dependence that can be unhealthy. It also easily generates tensions when differences in social background intensify the situation. Resolution and working together require addressing nuance, not just in college sports but in wider social relations. Latrell Scott's quick action showed that he grasped the dynamic. I am grateful.

Given the complexity of all that was happening, my life off the field and outside the classroom was limited. The pursuit of success can breed isolation. I was seeking balance in my life, but I had not found it. After all, I was at Richmond for one reason: football success. I did what was needed in the classroom, allowing me to focus on my game. There was little time for anything else, especially relationships.

Briefly, there was a girl on the track team who intrigued me. I began to spend some time with her. She seemed to want a relationship. Then, one day, casually and with no warning she said something that startled me. "You're so confident about football. What if it doesn't work out?" It was a natural question for two people getting to know one another. But to me, it was jolting, a challenge to my sense of purpose, to my identity, to all that I had. I was not ready for this challenge. I heard her words as someone telling me what I could not do, who I could not be. Immediately I lost interest in her. It was a kind of emotional reflex. I had no further contact with her. If anybody was against what I wanted to be, where I wanted to go, I cut them off.

While I was a student at Richmond, I met Rikki, who would become my wife. We met in my sophomore year. She was a student at Virginia Commonwealth University (VCU), a large urban school, virtually the opposite of the University of Richmond. We met through a mutual friend and, at first, I assumed she was his girlfriend. I was in awe. Immediately I saw that she was confident, intelligent, sincere, and kind. She fit in with various people, warmly, easily. At first, I was very taken with her. I could not stop thinking about it. But I hesitated. Time passed and I did not see her again.

My soul and my mind were intensely focused. Meanwhile, gradually, the University of Richmond was broadening my perspective. I was discovering all sorts of unfamiliar people and ideas. New thoughts began to reshape my assumptions. I was forced to ask what was true and why it was true. I learned to ask probing questions and to face the reality of dealing with people who were different, in what they believed and how they lived.

Even with the overriding goal of football success, my perspective on life became wider and deeper at Richmond. Even the tensions within me were evidence of development, of maturity.

Aleta Richards saw all of this clearly. She had been a faculty member at Episcopal High School and she and her husband, Bob Ellis, had been faculty residents in the dormitory. They also own a house near the University of Richmond where I was able to stay in the summer before my senior year. Staying near campus allowed me to be near the football team's training facilities. "Letting Tim use our house was one of the best decisions Bob and I have ever made," Aleta readily says. Now I call Aleta and Bob my godparents. We began to speak honestly, candidly. She has been a counselor and holds a doctorate. She has good insights and has been a great support. "Tim is a problem-solver," she emphasizes. She knows how determined I can be!

In one respect my development was clear. During my senior year, I found Rikki again. Another friend encouraged me and this time nothing could stop. We traded texts and quickly became inseparable. We did everything possible together. She would become the first and the last person I talked to every day. The relationship quickly deepened and left me with a feeling like I had never had. Being with her took away much of my stress. I felt accepted, heard, understood. I tried to give back in the same way. My life changed. I found new parts of myself.

Rikki remembers those Richmond years vividly. "What stood out was Tim's determination. You knew he dreamed big. I remember thinking, 'This guy is a trip!' If you challenged his intention, you risked becoming invisible to him. He would just walk away. But by his senior year, it was clear that he was discovering himself."

My years at Richmond did not end exactly as I and my teammates hoped. In my senior year, the fall of 2007, we were 11–2, going into a Division I playoff game against Appalachian State at their stadium in Boone, North Carolina. I was suffering from a sprained MCL (medial cruciate ligament) in the knee and was not at full speed. I managed to gain ninety-five yards on twenty-two carries. But we lost to Appalachian, 35–55. It was my last college game, and it was a disappointment given how far we had come and how much I had progressed.

Before leaving Richmond, I made a point of going to see Coach Clawson. It was a fitting goodbye, after one of the last practices. "Just think," I said to him, "you don't have to deal with me again." Clawson did not back down. "And you don't have to deal with me." Our standoff had become polite, even humorous. I learned much as a Richmond Spider. Now it was time for the National Football League. I remained convinced that no one and nothing could prevent me from reaching success there.

Chapter Seven

ONE DUFFLE BAG

What you need for the journey is already inside you.

At 7:30 one morning, late in my senior year at Richmond, the phone rang. It was the football team's trainer. "A coach wants to see you," he said simply. It was not just any coach. It was an assistant coach from an NFL team. I threw on some clothes and dashed off from my room in the dorm to see who this might be.

In a sense, this was no surprise. It was "pro day" at the University of Richmond. A group of NFL scouts and coaches would evaluate various college players they were considering for the upcoming draft—when professional teams would select promising new players. Once again, I was down to one opportunity, in this case one event, to prove myself. I would have to show exceptional strength and speed with coaches studying every move I made. I would be measured against the very best players, nothing less. It was exciting and it was nerve-wracking.

The pressure was even greater because I had not been selected for the NFL "Combine." Each spring a few athletes are invited to a week-long set of evaluations by NFL coaches and scouts. The extent of the event and the presence of all the teams ensure a thorough process of consideration. Those who have been saying it is a grind. But I wasn't invited. I couldn't understand why I was left out. I was one of the best running backs at the I-AA level of college football. I was a finalist for the Walter Payton Award for excellence as a collegiate running back. My teammate Arman Shields was invited to the Combine, but I was not. I didn't get it. I was angry. What more could I do?

I had proven I was capable. I had proven I was reliable. I had become a team leader, someone to whom people turned, a model of determination. I set the tone in the locker room and on the field. What more could I do?

Left out of the Combine, I went back to work, back to conditioning with fresh conviction. My instinct then was to find a specialized trainer. The pro day at Richmond became my chance. Specific abilities would be tested in only one day. I had to perform then and there. I had to show my ability to handle mental and physical pressure. There are specialized facilities that prepare players for the Combine or for a pro day. I couldn't afford that. Instead, I chose a special trainer who would get me ready.

It seemed like the right thing to do. But I should have stuck with Coach Horgan, my trainer at the university. He knew me. He had a vested interest in me. We could have made quick progress. Looking back, I learned a basic lesson: stick with who knows you and what you know best. I was on the verge of NFL consideration; I should have kept the trainer and the program that got me to that point.

I did not make a bad decision; but, it was not the best decision. The specialty coach worked me hard. However, I got too bulky, building up too much muscle. Later I realized that a player needs to be light and lean for pro day. The right combination of strength and agility fill the bill. As the day drew near, I did not feel right. I did not feel fully ready. It was the big day, my best shot at being drafted by an NFL team. I would have been nervous anyway. So, not feeling right physically intensified the nervousness. My mind was spinning with these thoughts when I learned, at 7:30 in the morning, that a coach wanted to see me, right away.

I soon located Maurice ("Mo") Carthon, an assistant coach with the Arizona Cardinals. As a player, Carthon had been to the Super Bowl with the New York Giants when they were coached by Bill Parcells. Like his mentor, Carthon represented old-school, tough football. Never one for many words, he had a simple message for me. He had watched film of my games. He liked what he saw. My style reminded him of Curtis Martin, the great running back of the New York Jets. As a result, Carthon said in a matter-of-fact way, the Cardinals planned to draft me.

I should have been elated. But nervous uncertainty took over. OK, it was Carthon, a great player and now an assistant coach. He had just told me the Cardinals planned to draft me. In other words, I would be invited to the National Football League. At the time, I could not grasp this message. Was this credible? I had nervously focused on performing for pro day. That was still in front of me. I had to show exceptional ability. I could not let up. Why would Carthon say this before pro day began? What if I blew it? It was job day with the NFL. I could not lose focus.

Later I would realize the importance of mental as well as physical preparation. The shape my mind was in mattered as much as the condition my body had achieved. On that day, even with Carthon's surprising news, I was on edge. It was not good. I had even run out of money to pay my cell phone bill and had to negotiate an extension with the phone company. Things were tense. Just when you need things to work, to be right, it always seems like something breaks or distracts you, challenging the focus you need.

The cell phone issue was one more reminder of how fragile, how tenuous, my life was. It reminded me of where I had come from and what I was striving to achieve. Just because you live in the ghetto, my mother used to say, the ghetto doesn't have to live in you. In other words, you don't have to be confined by your surroundings. Take care of yourself and reach for more than you currently are. At an early age, I learned to present myself at my very best.

To perform at your best, especially when the stakes are high, you have to put your mind in the right space. This requires the right kind of tension, a creative tension. Later, after I began to grasp this idea, the right kind of tension would serve me well through four years of recovery and rehabilitation. It would be one of the most valuable lessons I would learn.

On pro day at Richmond, however, I was not quite there. When the strength and speed drills began I was so nervous that I was literally shaking. I did twenty reps on the bench press knowing I should have done more. The day became a blur. Fortunately, to some extent, my mind and body shifted to natural instincts and abilities. As best I could, I used my experience and gifts. But I had never felt such a challenge as I felt that day. I did not do as well as I hoped.

Life lessons were coming at me hard and fast. Stick with what got you there. Be in the moment. Communicate what you need. Be mentally as well as physically ready. I tried to absorb it all. But I could not stop thinking, and worrying, about where I wanted my life to go: to be drafted by an NFL team. I didn't trust what I had heard. Carthon's words had yet to come true.

The NFL draft is an annual event in the spring where each of the league's teams selects new players. They will be rookies, most from the college ranks, entering professional football for the first time. Each team receives a chance to select a player in an order that reverses the prior season's final standings. The teams with better won-loss records draft toward the end of each round, after teams with mediocre to poor records. The draft is organized by rounds over several days. On occasion, a team will trade its slot to acquire a player already in the league. Nationally televised, the draft is avidly watched by fans. Speculation about who will be drafted by which team can consume sports gossip for weeks prior to the draft. The draft's earlier rounds attract greater interest because more highly touted players tend to be drafted first.

Anticipating being drafted, hopefully sooner rather than later, I gathered my parents, my fiancé Rikki, and my godmother, Aleta Richards, who had become a valued counselor and friend since my years at Episcopal High School. We were together at a hotel in Richmond, anxiously and impatiently watching as the draft proceeded and names were called. But my name was not among them. The first day of the draft ended without my name being called.

It was the year of the running back. In this 2008 draft, twenty-three running backs were chosen among 252 players drafted overall. Perhaps twenty of those running backs would soon be starters for their teams. At the time none of that would not have mattered to me. All I knew was that I had not been chosen on the first day. I was angry, upset. For once it was not clear what I could do. I was not in control. It was not clear what would happen. I could only resolve to stay present, to manage my expectations as best I could. It was what I had worked for since I was a kid. Now all I could do was wait. It was agony.

Then it happened. Our group had gone to a sports bar in the Glen Allen area of suburban Richmond. The dynamics were not ideal. My parents were not pleased with Rikki and Aleta being there. There was a sense of parental prerogative, of not wanting to share me with others in such a glorious moment. It was a dynamic that would surface again and again. We were all trying to behave, but it was tense. Food and the noise of a sports bar helped a bit.

In the middle of our meal my cell phone, the bill having been paid, rang. It was Ken Whisenhunt, coach of the Arizona Cardinals. "You're our next pick," he said. Then Maurice Carthon got on the line. "I told you we were going to draft you. Be ready to get to work." Then he hung up.

Word spread quickly through the sports bar. People came up for autographs. Some wanted me to sign jerseys. That felt good. I had worked hard for so long. There was some relief.

There also was nuance. I was realizing that life is more than any one of us. I was part of something larger. My actions had made an impact on others. The happy scene in the sports bar became a vivid reminder. People wanted to share the moment of joy.

For the time being, I could not celebrate. All I thought about was going to work out. Why can't you celebrate, people would ask me at various times in my life? Now it is clear there was fear of losing, an insecurity that prevented me from relaxing. I told myself that I had nowhere to turn, that I had to keep in control, keep pushing, keep striving to achieve more and more. This drive had taken me a long way. Eventually, I would find that there are limits. Highs are followed by lows, even by the risk of crashing. For the time being, I was thrilled to have been drafted and was ready to get to work, as Maurice Carthon insisted.

In life, hopefully, there are moments of triumph. Even more, there are likely to be small points of growth and advance. We share those times, if we are fortunate, with people who embrace our hopes in depth. Aleta Richards taught me this lesson. It would become even more valuable over the next few years. Eventually, I would learn how to celebrate.

As these realizations took shape in my life, time moved quickly. In just a few months it was time to report to the Arizona Cardinals. Rookie players reported a month before the mini-camp for veterans began. So, in May, off I went to Phoenix. It would be another transition after a lifetime of transition. When I was a kid, my family had moved again and again, crossing the continent. We had also faced involuntary transitions such as evictions. Most of the transitions I had experienced were more negative than positive. We had to move away from, not just toward, a new situation. Of course, when I entered Episcopal and later Richmond, the sense of promise was large. As my football ability blossomed and I gained recognition, transitions became filled with hope. Now, leaving Richmond for Arizona, the stakes had never been higher.

I will never forget the night before I left. There wasn't much to pack. I needed only one duffle bag for all of my things. It was hugely symbolic. One duffle bag. I was learning that I did not need a lot of possessions. What I needed most was already inside me. I had accumulated much already, in terms of life's lessons. The most important things that went with me to Arizona were the direction, focus, and determination I had cultivated. This was the transition of which I had dreamed, for which I had worked. I was going to play football with the best. But there was so much more I could not have anticipated.

The full training camp, with veteran players and rookies, would be later, in July, in Flagstaff, Arizona. Located over one-hundred-forty miles north of Phoenix, Flagstaff sits at nearly 7,000 feet above sea level. Its summer weather is mild compared to the scorching desert heat of the Cardinals' home, making Flagstaff an appealing place to train. Even in May, morning workouts for the rookies in Phoenix were in 100-degree heat. It was like nothing I had ever felt, part of this major transition that was hitting me all at once. Another symbol of my new life was the large playbook I had to digest, the notebook containing all of the Cardinals' plays and formations. I was a pro now; it was my job to learn that book.

A lot was coming at me and the greater challenge was off the field. Where would I live in Phoenix? At first, this was a moot point. For the rookie camp, the team fed us and put us up at a hotel. We were shuttled back and forth to the training facility. It was all football, leaving little time for anything else but sleep. The distance, physical and emotional, did not sit well with people who were used to having ready access to me, my family, and close friends. The cell phone would ring but I would not hear it or I could not talk. My life was changing, and people close to me did not like it. This dynamic would intensify as my place on the Cardinals' roster became firm. I was doing well on the practice field. Otherwise, looking back, I was not doing so well.

An example that had arisen, and would come up over and over, was money. Through rookie camp, housed and fed by the team, there was little need for money. But I was anxious to sign a contract. I was the first of the Cardinals' rookies to sign a contract when offered one later in the summer. Most rookie salaries are more or less fixed within a range. The signing bonus is more variable, based on the round in which a player was drafted. My signing bonus was $186,000 before taxes, which took a 40 percent hit. I could not believe how much had been taken when I finally saw the check. Still, it was more money than I had ever seen, by far.

I felt proud, felt the hard work was all worth it. but I knew nothing about finance. I had plunged into a new world. But mentally, I was not there. There were things I had to prove given where my life had been. I went to a grocery store and bought ten boxes of cereal simply because I could do that. Most of the cereal later went stale. I bought a car, a used Lexus, and later realized I had accepted an 18 percent finance rate. I went to a mall and bought clothes. For a month I had lived out of one duffle bag. Life's lessons were piling up. It was astonishing, at times embarrassing, to see how much there was to do, how much to be understood with little time to process it all. There was far more to life than showing up and playing football, although that had been the mental image I carried. I needed guidance.

For the full training camp, we gathered in the third week of July at Northern Arizona University, in Flagstaff, staying in the dormitories and using their athletic facilities. It almost felt like being back in Richmond. But this proved to be total immersion in football of a higher caliber. By then my Richmond pride had been on full display. I remember ordering Richmond gear just to promote my school. I was in the midst of players from major schools that supply scores of professional players. I was determined to hold my own and to make Richmond proud.

It was tough. My physical condition was excellent. But it took my body a week to adjust to grueling training at the high altitude of Flagstaff. Plus, Maurice Carthon, the running backs coach who had secured my draft, was on me in every practice. He saw something in me and wanted to bring it out. His approach was to ride me hard, yelling, criticizing. He never said it, but clearly, he had become invested in my success. His approach was intensity and more intensity. Never letting me think I had done anything right.

Once the veterans reported, I also was in the midst of well-known professional players, several of whom would make the professional football Hall of Fame. Players such as Kurt Warner and Larry Fitzgerald were in the locker room with me. I was amazed to be there, but not overwhelmed. I became more determined. I was there to play football. I was there to represent Richmond. I held back a bit, not jumping to make friends. I did not want to lose focus. It did not dawn on me at first that I needed people to guide me on the field as well as off. That may have been my most difficult transition of all. I would need guidance.

By the 2008 NFL season, Edgerrin James was well on his way to pro football's Hall of Fame. In his first two seasons with the Indianapolis Colts, James won the league's rushing title for most yards gained running with the ball. It should not have been a surprise. At the University of Miami, he set rushing records and ranks as one of that college's best running backs ever.

James left the Colts after seven seasons to join the Arizona Cardinals. In his first two seasons in Phoenix, he rushed for over 1,000 yards in each season. The respect accorded James extended beyond the playing field. He is a player whom many admire for the extent of his contributions. I knew that and should have been grateful at first, as I was later, when James reached out to me. Looking back, it was amazing. "Stick with me," he said often. "I've got you," he emphasized. Consistently he followed through. He didn't want me by myself. When I pulled a hamstring muscle and thought I might miss practice, he helped me recover quickly. I went to camp thinking it was me against the world. I learned what words like "reliance" and "guidance" meant.

Edgerrin James remembers Tim, the rookie, vividly and warmly. "Tim was different, totally different, from most rookies." James recalls several attributes that he saw quickly. "He had to grind it out to get to the NFL. He was determined. He was focused and confident, but he learned that he needed guidance, unlike many rookies. I saw his motivation. He is the kind of person who draws others to him."

"How many kids wish they could be where Tim and I were," James reflects. "Those who do make it in the NFL often come from single-parent families, or little family at all. Sports becomes the other parent. It becomes the way out. Tim was unusual because he had both of his parents together, both pulling for him. That made his example even more powerful."

"Edge," as I soon called him, took care of me in so many ways. As training camp was about to break, I was told that I must host a lavish dinner at a fancy restaurant in suburban Scottsdale, Arizona. I assumed there would just be a few guys. "Edge" told me to make a reservation for twenty people and named one of the area's best restaurants. My head began to spin. It spun even more when I saw what people were ordering. I was still getting my head around new financial realities. I had never seen anything like the steady stream of expensive drinks and food passing among the group for whom I was footing the bill. It was scary.

Then, from across the restaurant, I received a text from "Edge." He knew. "Tim, I see you are sweating. Don't worry. I've got this." I agreed not to tell. It was amazing. He had covered me in an amazing way. I resolved to do that for younger players when I would have the chance. My eyes were opening. I could not fly solo. I would need guidance and I could give guidance. In just a few months, without knowing it until later, I had begun one of the greatest transitions every person must make: being part of a team off the field as well as on it. That lesson, and the sort of transitions that lift it up, would become more important when my place in football suddenly was threatened.

Chapter Eight

USE WHAT GOT YOU HERE

There are thirty-two teams in the National Football League, and I had made the roster of one of them, the Arizona Cardinals. It was a dream come true. Anyone who makes an NFL roster would be called a success by most people. In the fifth grade, I had scribbled on a piece of paper that I would become a professional football player and now I had done it. The journey had been a long one. I had moved through four high schools, two years at Episcopal High School topping the list. Only the University of Richmond, a smaller school, had offered me a football scholarship, and I had been a fifth-round pick in the NFL draft. In training camp, I had proven myself. Edgerrin James, an obvious choice for the Hall of Fame, had become my mentor and friend. From the outside looking in, I seemed to be on top of the world.

But I wanted more. I wanted the spotlight. I wanted to be one of the thirty-two starting running backs in the NFL. I had not reached professional football by waiting for my turn. I wanted more opportunities to be a starter, and I prepared for them with increased determination. We were doing well as a team, but I needed more. It was becoming a struggle to find balance between the high level of personal achievement I intended and the overall good of the team.

It seemed that circumstances were going my way. But while the team gained momentum on the field and focused on making the playoffs, there were tensions in the locker room. Our quarterback, Kurt Warner, preferred one style of play, whereas Edgerrin preferred another style. Despite the statistics being in Edge's favor, the coaching staff aligned with Warner. Edge did not hold back his disappointment. Tensions increased. As I had played better with each game, the coaches decided to promote me to starter at running back over Edge. I had never imagined that getting to the role I had coveted would become so complicated.

As excited as I was about the opportunity, something did not feel right. Edge had been playing well. Why were the coaches benching him? Were they pitting him against me? Were they punishing him for his vocal displeasure with the team's new direction? Edge had become more than a teammate. He had become a big brother, a mentor. Is there ever a right way or time to surpass your mentor? Would our relationship change? Would he resent me? Would this affect his Hall of Fame chances? I wanted the opportunity, but not at his expense. New questions assailed me. It would hardly be the last time.

Fortunately, Edge put these concerns to rest. "Congrats man," he said, "You earned it. Go make the most of this opportunity. Don't worry about me. I've been there. I understand this business. I'll be OK." Instinctively I realized these were not just words. If he says something, you can trust it. I realized that his role modeling for me was continuing in a new and substantial way.

I took Edge's words to heart. I soon had rushed for 122 yards and scored two touchdowns in my first game. Our 34–10 victory over the Rams was a high point. But that high would not last. I struggled to maintain the level of performance I expected of myself. I was demanding more and more from my body. This meant more time was needed in treatment to recover. There also was more study of game films to prepare and more reps in practice. In my mind, I expected more of myself, and I could feel Cardinals' fans also wanting more from me. Looking back, it was inevitable that I would begin to fade, physically and mentally.

Less than a year had passed since I had been drafted and left Richmond. The demands had grown steadily, especially as the NFL season ground ahead. It was taking its toll. None of the pressures and expectations had eased. If anything, they had increased. I struggled to adapt. I had not fully absorbed the sophisticated kind of teamwork that was required, nor the steady routine needed to develop it. In addition, late in the season, the Cardinals had begun to struggle, losing some close games, then getting blown out by the New England Patriots, 7–47. In order to keep playoff hopes alive, the coaches brought Edge back as the starter at running back. Mentally I was a wreck. Had I lost the opportunity for which I fought? Would I ever be trusted with that role again? I had never gone backward, always moving ahead. It was a hard lesson.

It was slowly dawning on me that my habits of mind needed to match the level of my physical preparation. My temptation was to hide, not to go out in public. I was reluctant to ask for help. It seemed like an admission of failure. I had put all of my effort into getting there, reaching the top. I had not readied myself for the highs and lows, and for the sheer demands of staying there, staying on top of my game. I needed to bounce back and do so quickly without feeling sorry for myself.

Slowly I began to open up, to adapt, and to let the people closest to me into what was going on. If working with others, especially family and close friends, got me here, then that was what I needed to do again. I was forced to admit that isolation and self-criticism, even bouts of self-loathing, were destructive. I started staying later at practice with coach Mo Carthon. I spent more time with Edge, again asking him questions, and gave more time to the weight room.

To my surprise, people were not judging me. They proved to be even more of a support system than I had imagined. Once I made the first move, they respected my new transparency and saw my determination to be better, to learn. "I've had rough days," Edge shared. "You are never going to be the biggest, strongest, fastest; there will always be someone better. You have to learn how to manage the bad days. Everyone has them, some manage them better than others."

How do you manage the lows in your life? "You stick to your routine, focusing on the fundamentals." In other words, use what got you here. "When your body is hurting, don't try to do too much, don't fight your body." Edge went on to explain that there is something called the rookie wall. It is when your mind and body finally catch up with all that you have done and start to become burned out. All the highs of pro day and the draft and training camp and the actual season. All the lows of physical demands and starting then not starting. Adrenaline carries you a long way. With everything coming at you, there is no time to rest, reflect, or take a break.

At some point, the initial rush wears off and you feel physically and emotionally drained. Some players begin to miss home or family and friends. Others feel overwhelmed with the flood of new people in their lives whom they must trust. My lifestyle had changed, a reality that would become clear later. For the moment, facing pressure like I had never felt, there proved to be a way forward. John Lott, my strength coach, echoed Edge's words. Use what got you here. Lott gave me workouts to build my body back heading into the final stretch of the season. He encouraged me to get more rest and to make use of chiropractic and massage therapy. The stress eased. My mood shifted. My passion for the game reignited.

As a team we closed out the season at 9–7, winning the division and making it to the playoffs, where we hosted a playoff game at home for the first time since 1947. With our new team slogan, "Shock the World," we were ready to make a Super Bowl run. I focused by cutting off all distractions. I spent more time with Edge, learning as much as I could. Our team success led us to the NFC championship game, against the Philadelphia Eagles, the biggest game in the history of the Cardinals to that point. There were 71,000 people in the University of Phoenix Stadium that afternoon. I had never experienced anything like it. As I looked around the stadium all I saw was a sea of red or white as fans wore red t-shirts or waved white towels in support of the home team. I was a long way from the University of Richmond, but I was ready for this moment. With the guidance of Edge, Mo Carthon, Lott, and teammates, I felt the best I had felt since my start against the Rams almost two months prior.

We jumped out to a 24–6 lead by halftime. Silence filled our locker room as we realized our advantage. We were two quarters away from the first Super Bowl in franchise history.

"Stay focused," Edge told me. "Remember your fundamentals. Let's finish this game." He was right. The game was far from over as the Eagles fought back to take the lead at 25–24 in the fourth quarter. Up until this point, I had contributed but had not been a focal point. Edge was coming off a shoulder injury in the previous game and was not at his best. Our offensive coordinator called on me going down the stretch. As I jogged to the huddle, I knew the game was on the line. It was fourth down with one yard to go for a first down. In my mind, Edge's words practically shouted at me: trust your fundamentals. Then Kurt Warner called an off-tackle run for me to carry the ball. I was shocked. With the season on the line and three veteran pro bowl players on offense, the Cardinals trusted the fifth-round draft choice from Richmond. Just weeks ago, I had been benched and begun to doubt myself. Suddenly I was in the biggest moment of the franchise's history.

Use what got you here, I told myself. Tim, this is what you prepared for. I thumped my chest twice and pointed up to the sky, "Thank you, God." The play was designed to run off tackle, but as the ball was hiked, I saw an opening to the outside. I went off script to dash for the sideline, breaking a tackle and picking up the first down. My adrenaline was at an all-time high. I wanted the ball, I wanted more. Two plays later, on third down, my number was called, and I delivered again. Then it was third and goal on the Eagles' eight yard-line. Although we trailed by one point, I was in a zone. Again, Kurt Warner called my number. It was a screen pass to the left. Everyone would expect the ball to go to one of our two pro bowl receivers on offense, Larry Fitzgerald or Anquan Boldin. The play was designed to fake the pass to both of them while I slipped to the other side of the field.

When the ball was snapped, I did just as I had practiced so often. As I caught the ball I turned toward the goal, hesitating briefly to allow my linemen to get in front of me. Then I headed straight for the goal line with an intention that would not be denied. As I approached the goal line, I felt a hit from each side, and then someone grabbed my legs. My body twisted and turned as I fell to the ground. I got up and quickly looked to the sideline toward the referee. He raised both arms to signal a touchdown. Up to this point, I could hear nothing. My focus shut out crowd noise. Seeing the referee, I let out a scream, then heard the crowd roar. We had done it. We had taken the lead and were minutes away from our first Super Bowl appearance. When the final whistle blew, red and white confetti dropped from the ceiling. I fell to my knees, tears flooding my eyes. I had scored the winning touchdown to send the Cardinals to the Super Bowl.

I was overwhelmed with gratitude. What if I had given up on myself? What if the team gave up on me? As players, coaches and reporters stormed the field, I noticed my family rushing towards me. The excitement on their faces brought tears back to my eyes. Personal sacrifice always impacts more than just you.

Two weeks stood between the NFC championship and the Super Bowl. Television networks and people from all over the world anticipate the big game. My phone rang non-stop. College friends, coaches, teachers, and family members called to offer congratulations. It seemed as if every news station requested an interview. The first few days were exciting. I was soon to be a part of a unique class of players who have played in the Super Bowl. I wanted to enjoy it, but I refused to turn away from the vow I had made weeks earlier: stay focused, stick to your routine. Manage the lows and stay focused during the highs. The natural tendency is to relax. Enjoy the moment. You earned it. There were parties everywhere, everyone wants to connect with you. I remember signing twenty-five autographs in exchange for $5,000 cash. How do you stay focused in such a moment?

As we arrived in Tampa, one week before the Super Bowl, staying focused seemed impossible. As our team bus pulled up to the hotel, lines of fans wrapped around the corner of the building. news and sports media outlets crowded around. Everywhere you went and everything you did would be recorded and criticized on radio or television within minutes. The lack of privacy became overwhelming. Players searched for side and back entrances to sneak in and out of the hotel. We covered our heads with hoodies and our mouths when we spoke.

In an effort to maintain routine, I flew my chiropractor, stretch therapist, and massage therapist to Tampa for the week. Everything around me was different but I needed my body to perform the same. By media day, I realized the significance of this game. I sat on the podium and suddenly hundreds of reporters from all over the world rushed into the room. My words were being transmitted all over the world. It was amazing. But it was another distraction. I could not lose focus. The game could not come soon enough.

As I walked onto the field of Tampa's Raymond James Stadium and looked around, I felt like I was in a dream. As a kid, I often simulated playing in the Superbowl. I would sit in my bed at night visualizing what it would feel like to walk through the tunnel, have all eyes on me, and score the winning touchdown. Stepping on the field felt like a dream realized. How many kids had this same dream? Yet I had gotten a chance to live it. For once I embraced my path that led me to this point. All of the mistakes, not being big, fast, or good enough. Four different high schools, the injuries, and even the days I doubted myself. None of it mattered now. Here I was. It was my path and it led me here. It's hard to see the beauty in your journey until you get to where you're going. What if I had given up? What if I lost hope?

Suddenly I snapped back to reality. There was a very big game to play. I needed to warm up to get ready to go. The game seemed like a blur. I never really let go. I was so tense, so focused on not messing up. I did not enjoy the game. You work so hard for the biggest opportunity only to forget to enjoy the moment.

Back and forth we battled against the Steelers. Next thing I knew I was watching Larry Fitzgerald catch a pass and race sixty-five yards to take the lead with less than, two minutes to go. As our offense jogged off the field, we stood on the sideline watching, knowing there was nothing more we could do. We needed one stop from our defense to make history. I watched as Pittsburgh moved down the field gaining first down after first down and then came a play I will never forget.

It was third and goal. Pittsburgh's quarterback, Ben Roethlisberger, rolled out to his right and threw the ball to Santonio Holmes as he tip-toed into the corner of the end zone. One referee signaled touchdown while the other signaled incomplete. The video review showed it was a touchdown. I tried to blink, hoping it was a nightmare, One instant changed history. My body went numb. I could not make sense of what happened. Would we be remembered as the greatest team in Cardinals' history, or the team who lost to the Steelers in the Superbowl?

It was difficult to rebound from such a devastating loss. We had come so close, only to lose on a late touchdown that required video review. Everywhere I went in the next few months, family and friends, and people in the public, just wanted to talk about the Super Bowl. I suppose I was their window on an event they hoped they could be a part of through me. Even though the Cardinals lost to the Steelers, people still wanted to celebrate my having gone to the Super Bowl.

My mind was elsewhere. I was in no mood to celebrate. Less than a year before, the Cardinals had drafted me. On that night, I had thought of little but going to work out, gearing up for an even higher level of performance. After the Super Bowl, I wanted to look ahead. There were troubling questions about my place on the Cardinals. What role would I have going forward? It was unclear. I had set a record for touchdowns scored by a rookie, but I had been benched late in the season. I wanted to invest in the Cardinals, but did the Cardinals want to invest in me? There were troubling signs. Maurice Carthon who had recruited me left for a coaching spot on another team. It made me wonder. I resolved to train even more, even harder.

Then it seemed as if the question had been answered in the worst possible way. In the NFL draft for 2009, the year after I had been drafted, the Cardinals chose Beanie Wells, a running back from Ohio State, in the first round. That sent a message, and I was infuriated. I knew that professional football is intensely competitive with no guarantees. I was also starting to learn that it is a business. The Cardinals invested in Beanie Wells. That meant less of an investment in me. They wanted a return on their investment. That meant Wells was groomed to be the player I had intended to be. The opportunity to be the franchise player, the starting running back, seemed to be fading.

In the short run, I reverted to form. I became more competitive. I also concluded that I was tougher and smarter than Beanie. He is a valued friend now. Then, he was the one I was determined to outshine. I believed that the best performance on the field was all that mattered. I resolved to work harder and do better. I had faced such challenges before. I would overcome them again.

I was hitting my stride as a player while Beanie struggled. But the Cardinals' focus on him remained clear. In a game against the Raiders, I played well but kept being replaced by Beanie. I lost my cool. A deep frustration set in. It seemed like no amount of effort, on and off the field, was good enough.

One thing I could do—and began to do during my rookie year—was to build my own support team. I created a group that included a massage therapist, holistic medicine doctor, chiropractor, and exercise specialist. Many players do this, spending well beyond $100,00 a year to keep in the peak of conditioning. "Edge" James urged me to make my body my main investment. He was right. Whatever strengthened me would likely lengthen my career.

There were times when I relied more on my own support team than on the Cardinals' medical staff. When I broke a thumb in a game against Tennessee, the coaching staff wanted to put me on the injured reserve list. I refused. The next game would be on Sunday night against the Minnesota Vikings with Brett Favre as their quarterback. No way I would miss that game! I confronted the coaches and insisted on being in the game plan. In the end, a special cast allowed me to play against the Vikings. I would never give up. I would prove my resilience.

But I could not rely solely on myself. I was learning to trust others for guidance. Just to find the right specialists to ensure peak conditioning, I asked seasoned players who they would recommend. It was part of awakening to the business side of football. At times, I even had to fire people I had hired because the arrangement was not working out. Young athletes entering football and other professional sports in their early twenties are thrown into unforeseen challenges and tough decisions. How can they handle it? I was fortunate to have knowledgeable teammates like "Edge" and Larry Fitzgerald as mentors on the Cardinals. Where would I have been without them? The tensions that arose on the field were being matched, and at times, overshadowed by tensions off the field. There were more lessons to be learned and they were intensely personal.

Chapter Nine

CHANGE OR REMAIN THE SAME?

As great as the tensions on the field were becoming in Arizona, they could hardly compare with the tensions arising off the field. Just as I was learning that professional football is a business, I was learning that my life itself had become something of a business. People wanted things from me. People even expected things from me. This was especially true of some people who were closest to me, those to whom I already felt some natural obligation. It's complicated, so let me explain.

"Beware of what you become in pursuit of what you want."
(Jim Rohn)

I should have seen it coming back at the sports bar in Richmond when the large-screen television announced that I had been drafted by Arizona. People soon found me and wanted autographs and pictures. My parents, my girlfriend Rikki, and my godmother Aleta, all beamed with pride. I became a public figure with name recognition. Once I made the Cardinals' roster, I was paid more than most people earn and more than my family had ever imagined. The dream was coming true, but dreams have consequences beyond what anyone can control.

It should have been clear to those closest to me that there would be other NFL players who would be paid more money, some far more. Add to that the competitive nature of the game. My spot on the roster was coveted by many athletes and could be gone in an instant. I would experience that when I was injured. It could all end in an instant, with no guarantees, only the prospect of more training, rehabilitation, and competition. That would become clear later.

These realities were not so clear to anyone else. Even to family and close friends, the image of the wealthy, revered athlete was uppermost in their minds. It seemed that everyone wanted something from me, starting with sheer access. My parents wondered aloud why I was less accessible, why I didn't just answer my phone, even if I was at practice or a team meeting. My parents also wondered openly why Rikki, increasingly the love of my life, got such access to me when they felt denied. They were even more dubious about Aleta, my godmother and guide since Episcopal High School.

Hadn't they raised me, they reasoned? Hadn't they sacrificed for me and their other children? Hadn't they groomed me and encouraged me and stood by me? Hadn't they held their marriage together for the sake of their family and the futures of their children? Their gifts to us have been huge. But my parents could not contain their suspicions of other people, who seemed like late-comers to the party. Even when I flew them to Cardinals' games, for which I also had to buy tickets, they were not placated. They knew I also flew Rikki to games. For them, this was a conflict of interest. It compromised whatever I did for them. It seemed I could never do enough. The result was that I began to feel fragmented and over-extended.

As I gained more recognition on the field, I received more demands off the field. One of my sisters, Qiana, had a car that constantly needed repair. I tried to help. My brother, Emmanuel, with no prior ties to Arizona, came to Phoenix and moved into the apartment I had rented. Later, Arman Shields, my college teammate and friend, also moved in. Arman had been drafted by the NFL's Raiders, actually chosen ahead of me. But there had been injuries and his career never really began. Like Emmanuel, Arman looked to me for space in which to regroup. How could I say no? What else could I do?

Soon the situation with Emmanuel worsened. I gave him a car that I acquired through an arrangement with a car dealer in Phoenix. His presence became a frustrating situation to maintain. One car did not manage his expectations that were getting out of control. In a way, it was nothing new, just the continuation of a life-long competition between us. Even playing sports as kids, we ended up fighting. Emmanuel was more artistic, talented, and outgoing. But I became more driven; my desire to win took over. I figured if I could beat my older brother, I could beat anyone. It became almost a mantra. He sensed my thoughts and resented them.

As we got older, there was a shift in our relationship. People assumed I was the older brother. Coaches took more notice of me. Our departure from DeMatha High School and my arrival in a private school were the final straws. The opportunities were increasing for me while Emmanuel's chance for a college athletic scholarship seemed to fade. Then he started to hang out with a different circle of friends and got into trouble. I saw his struggle, but I could not empathize. I had my own, increasing challenges.

Why couldn't Emmanuel understand? Even more, as I gained success on the football field, why couldn't he celebrate what I was achieving? Looking back, I wish I had been more aware. I had no clue what it was like for him, with a younger brother in whose shadow he had begun to live. I became so focused on getting where I wanted to be that I stopped being a brother to Emmanuel. Instead, I pulled away. I saw him as jealous and wondered if I could trust him. Distance grew between us. When he came to Phoenix, the tension and distance increased.

It was not so complicated with my sisters. Victoria and I were the closest. The youngest of the four of us, she and I had entered Episcopal High School together. We had a special connection. Qiana, the oldest sibling, was not into sports. She and I had no natural connection. At times we clashed, largely because she was determined to be the leader of the pack. We lived in different worlds that I increasingly could do little to bridge.

The feeling of losing control became relentless and I did not like it. It went beyond family. "Old" friends popped up, wanting something or just searching for some NFL gossip, names, or news they could drop with friends. I was feeling used. But with people I cared about, what was I supposed to do?

I was forced to draw some hard conclusions. It was becoming clear that the realities of my family and friends were not my realities. We were living in different worlds. This could be said to me as an accusation, like I had let people down. But I had to learn to say "no," to set boundaries, to be ready to disappoint expectations.

This was difficult. For years, I was driven by my determination to provide for my family. I did not want to see my parents struggle. I wanted to make my siblings proud. I never thought about the impact of my assumptions. I never asked what my family expected of me; I assumed I knew. Since we had grown up with so little money, I assumed money would solve everything and I was determined to earn that money. But as I realized my efforts were not appreciated as I had imagined, I began to pull back. The result was that I began to resent my family and they began to resent me.

It could have been worse, I suppose. One of my teammates' entire family moved in with him as soon as he was drafted. He was grateful to be able to help. But their demands were over the top. It did not feel right coming home from work, sacrificing his body every day, only to find his siblings asleep on the couch in the middle of the day. Eventually, he had enough and moved to his own private apartment. There he could focus on the game while family members continued to tap his resources.

I was climbing a steep learning curve. The experience expanded the meaning of being resilient, which injury and recovery later would dramatically expand. It was difficult to make changes in my outlook, in how I viewed people I cared about. It was just as difficult to grasp that football is more than a game. Players must build their careers on the field. But off the field, they do not enter downtime. It can be just as intense, and complex. The psychological pressure never eases, while the physical pressure has respites. I had built a team of specialists to tend to my body. In the family and public arenas, I was still learning how to respond.

Looking back, it was a search for personal balance. I began working with Charles Maka, a specialized personal trainer in

Phoenix. As Charles remembers it now, the workouts, often five times a week, became more than physical exercise.

Charles remembers those sessions vividly. "When he first came in, Tim assumed that only more was better. I was struck: he would do three times the workouts most players did. I tried to teach him that too much is detrimental. He wanted to be in better shape. But that is not just a matter of demanding more of one's body."

Charles' approach was to train the brain. That is, he wanted to bring mental instincts and body response into balance. "He began to learn that quality is not just defined by quantity. Quality comes from focus, and even from discomfort. We only totally grow as human beings in the midst of discomfort. But the discomfort is as much mental as it is physical."

Balance was becoming the key. So was trust. I began to trust Charles and to have open conversations with him. He had a great deal to say about finding opportunities, and success and failure that would serve me well after the injury. "I told Tim that there are times when we are not successful, but that does not mean we have failed. We only fail if we stop, and that means that failure is as much mental as it is physical. We can only learn when we are unsuccessful. Then we must press on." I would not fully appreciate this wisdom until later.

Fortunately, as I worked and discussed with Charles, Rikki and Aleta also showed the way. Rikki naturally understood and spoke openly. Aleta was a most unlikely friend. When she showed interest in how I was doing at Episcopal, I resisted. Does she think I'm needy? Why does she want to know how I'm doing? But soon it became clear that Aleta and her husband Bob were safe space. She knew little about sports. Yet she opened up new worlds of reading and learning. Even more, she asked questions and taught me to ask, about life, about values, about faith. A high level of trust developed, more trust than I had ever imagined.

When I came back East, I often flew into Richmond, to see Rikki, and to check in with Aleta and Bob. My parents didn't understand. What's in it for her, they wondered, especially as my professional career unfolded. But Aleta never over-stepped. It was always about listening, asking thoughtful questions, understanding. She was one of very few people who consistently gave support. She could listen and not judge. She showed a pathway to healing that would be crucial when I went down with a knee injury while playing for Washington.

Meanwhile, as I learned to be a better person off the field, I also had to learn to be a better player on the field. That challenge never went away. In some ways, it became more intense. More than competition with Beanie Wells was involved. In my second year with the Cardinals, I fumbled four times. In my third year, I fumbled five times. My offensive coordinator, Todd Haley, reminded me that "every time you fumble, you take food out of the mouths of my five daughters. Either you find a way to hold onto the ball or I will find someone else who will." A stubborn injury to my right shoulder could be cited. I preferred to carry the ball on my right side. But no explanation ever is satisfactory. I had fumbled too much and that was a problem.

I worked to correct, to adapt, carrying a football constantly, on and off the field. I also worked to build the strength of that shoulder. It was a vivid reminder that no player can relax, no player can ease up on training and practicing. Constant repetition builds instinct, makes one have to think less. The game is so fast with little time to think or even to see what is going on. One must rely on "feeling" the situation and acting instinctively.

The average play in the NFL lasts four to six seconds. Fine-tuning what one does in such instants takes an entire career.

Even as I worked to develop on the field, it was difficult seeing myself as a different person off the field. Yet, as I tried, often in vain, to manage expectations, and to help as I was able, numerous people told me I was different. This message came across as criticism or at least disappointment because I had not done what someone else wanted. I had to become more organized in my personal life, especially in financial matters. As I've tried to say, I was not a bottomless resource, able to give large gifts often. I also emphasize that I felt over-extended, as much emotionally as financially.

I didn't spend money on huge cars or splashy jewelry. As Edgerrin James encouraged, I did spend money on personal care. If that seemed selfish to some, so be it. I invested in my well-being to enhance and lengthen my football career. I'm glad I did even if some around me did not understand and even were disappointed.

It was ironic that I also was becoming disappointed. Even as I worked to be the starting running back, the franchise player I had envisioned becoming. But I was hitting a ceiling. It was more than the Cardinals drafting Beanie Wells, or the issue of fumbles that I had worked to overcome. The Cardinals had defined me as a role player, someone who would play mostly in certain situations such as gaining short-yardage first downs. But I wanted more and was determined to achieve it. If not for the Cardinals, then I would be the key running back for another team, a team that appreciated my gifts.

Even as I neared the top, the place for which I worked in professional football, my judgment was becoming clouded. A skewed perspective on what matters in life did not arise with the injury that ended football for four years. Already, when the left knee was sound, there had been some unwise decisions.

Even as I dated Rikki, and we grew closer, I met a woman who had been a notable athlete herself. She also was very driven. There was much in common, or so it seemed. Suddenly I had two relationships. It was a dilemma.

I began to feel that something had to happen, there had to be a resolution. I could grasp that because I was impatient in my role with the Cardinals and wanted resolution there. The emotional pressure intensified. I felt torn, even raw. It was clear that I had to make a commitment. But how to know? I prayed and I waited for a sign.

I believe in signs. The trick, of course, is not knowing what they will be or when they will come. In this case, there were several signs, and I paid attention.

My mother had been trying to convince me to do a personal website. She had been investigating online. As an example meant to persuade me to have my own website, she pulled up a website that she thought was impressive. Amazingly, it was the website of this other woman, the athlete with whom I had gotten involved. My mother did not know. I did not tell her then. I simply left the room.

Was this a sign? I have wondered about signs for a long time. Or was this just a coincidence? If it was a sign, was I supposed to turn to this other woman and away from Rikki? What did it mean?

Looking back, it meant that I would have to decide. That I had the power to decide, to choose which was the right relationship. I did not have all of the answers. None of us ever know all that we need to know. But we have the power to choose, to make decisions that shape our lives going forward. It was scary.

Scared to have to choose. Wishing that a sign meant a clear message about what to do. Knowing that the sign that had been given was the need to decide.

In a basic, instinctive way, I knew that then. Seeing her website, quite by chance, was a sign that juggling two relationships did not work, could not work. There would have to be a choice, or circumstances would choose for me.

When I had gotten some space, I knew, more clearly than ever, that I was meant to be with Rikki. As if that was not enough, the next day, my situation in the NFL suddenly changed.

It happened during training camp for the 2011 season, the start of my fourth year in the NFL. Already it was an unusual time. There had been a lock-out of players from team training facilities as a new collective bargaining agreement was negotiated. We had to train on our own, then rush to camp as a new agreement between players and owners was reached.

Like other teams, the Cardinals had barely returned to training camp, when I received a phone call. It was Mike Shanahan, coach of Washington, then known as the Redskins. The message was stunning, music to my ears. "I'm trading for you," Shanahan said. "We can build the team around you." Then he added, "We need you in Washington tomorrow." My apartment in Phoenix was filled with stuff from three years in Arizona. But there was no time to pack. That would have to wait.

There was only time for one duffle bag. It had become symbolic of starting over, just like leaving Richmond to enter the NFL. Only the essentials were necessary, especially what was in my heart and my body, the training I had done to reach this point. The most important things to bring to Washington were determination and preparation.

After Shanahan called, Ken Whisenhunt, coach of the Cardinals, phoned. He wished me well. One door opens, another door closes. It was personal and yet it wasn't. Football is a business and decisions are made on that basis. For a moment I was sad. I had given a lot of myself to the Arizona Cardinals. Then I was glad. Phoenix is a big city, but it feels casual. "DC" is a big city, a world city. I had learned to feel at home in Phoenix, but the "DC" area was home. My family, my education, and my girlfriend were all in the vicinity. Plus, Shanahan made the promise I longed to hear. He would build the team around me. I heard the words over and over.

Leaving Phoenix proved to be much harder than leaving Richmond four years earlier. Emmanuel and Arman Shields still lived in my Phoenix apartment. They were not thrilled by news of the trade and my sudden departure. Their response drove home the harsh reality: we lived in different worlds. They were in search of themselves; I was on a fast track. So fast, there was only time to pack one duffle bag. Yet again, it wasn't a lot of things that were needed. All I truly needed was inside me. I would have to relearn that lesson sooner than I imagined.

In the end, Emmanuel and Arman had time to make their own arrangements. Meanwhile, even as I flew east, I was awakening to the impact my life was having on others. The focused determination to succeed as a professional athlete was not widely understood, yet it affected people around me. For the time being, I still could not see it clearly because the dream was nearing realization. They would build the team around me. Mike Shanahan's promise was not idle. By the sixth game of the season, Kyle Shanahan, offensive coordinator, told me at halftime that he was putting the game on my shoulders.

It was all coming true. I was reaching the place of my dreams, finally. I also had become clear in my heart and my mind about Rikki. I wanted to be with her. It seemed that everything was coming together. In just a few weeks I would be Washington's starter at running back as our team went to Charlotte, ready to secure a winning season and a spot in the NFL playoffs.

Who would have imagined that, in Charlotte, against the Carolina Panthers, I would be the starting running back for Washington, my home? At halftime, Kyle Shanahan would tell me that the game was on my shoulders. But as soon as it came together, it fell apart, more than I could ever have imagined.

It would have been impossible to predict that, a few minutes later into the game's second half, I would be unable to stand up, that I would be carried to the locker room, and would face surgery? Worse, who could have imagined that four years of recovery would follow, the injury never really being repaired, twisting my life like a pretzel? No one could have convinced me that I would fly back and forth across the country seeking answers. Or, that answers would surface, and I would recover. In the process, I would discover what words like "determination" and "resilience" meant. Even more, I would find myself and discover what it means to live.

Chapter Ten

LOSING MYSELF

Before I knew what was happening, I began to lose myself. Not only my injured knee but myself. The self I had worked hard to build ever since I was a kid. The self that only knew football. The self that had incredible focus and determination to succeed. I had come far. Then, in an instant, in a game in Charlotte, my left knee and my life began to fall apart.

There were signs that things would not be the same from the moment the injury occurred. Barely a day had passed since the injury when I saw my replacement at the Washington training facility. I was on crutches and could not play. He walked in, ready to go. Things are just that competitive. Things change just that fast. It's not personal, they say, it's business. But it is deeply personal.

I was ready for the competition. I always had been. I resolved to press ahead. When you're stressed, you go with what worked before. That meant fresh determination. I went ahead with the surgery then began extensive rehabilitation. Other players had done it, so I would do it. And I would do it better and faster. There's no substitute for determination. Little did I know what sort of determination would be needed.

The surgery and rehab were in Pensacola at the facility of a highly regarded surgeon who operated on many athletes. He declared the surgery a success and was certain the knee would heal. I settled in for an extensive program of healing and rebuilding strength in Florida. It was November 2011. The season was lost but I was still under contract to Washington. Preparation for the next season came into focus. There was time, if only the knee would respond.

But it didn't. The knee was not responding as it should. It remained stiff and swollen. Surely more rehab and exercise would resolve that. But nothing worked. Still there was time. Things could still get better.

I had overcome everything before. I would overcome this. So, there would be more effort, more work. But there were only modest results. Added to that, money soon became an issue. Before the injury, I had passed up an opportunity that seemed unnecessary at the time. Since I was entering my fourth year in the NFL as I joined Washington, my agent wondered if I should buy insurance for a "player unable to perform." If I paid $50,000 I would gain $4 million in coverage. I declined. Why take out insurance when I had never had an injury that put me out of action for long? If there was an injury, I reasoned, I would recover and likely make more than the policy would pay. That became a bad decision when I was injured with no prospect of a quick return to playing.

Yet once injured, as ever, I looked ahead. OK, the knee is taking longer. Don't worry, my mental voice spoke. The knee will come around. The surgeon sees no problem. All the right things are being done. It takes time. Meanwhile, I proposed to Rikki, and we began to plan a wedding. We got married in June 2012. I was hobbling, but it was almost time for training camp and life would get back on track. We rented a large home in Leesburg, Virginia, near the Washington training facility. I assumed I would be back on the team with a hefty contract. That was a faulty assumption. Bad decisions based on bad assumptions were doing me in.

The knee was not getting better. It remained swollen and sore. So once camp began, I doubled up on exercises and therapy, arriving before the sun was up each day. One morning, though, the trainer's phone rang and he looked toward me. "They want to see you in the office." Quickly I toweled off, dressed, and went. These were the first few steps on an awful journey.

I was told that I had been cut, let go, fired. I was physically unable to play, so the team dropped me. It was the worst moment of my life.

Football had been everything. Now it had been taken away, just like that. In an instant, like the knee injury itself. Only this was a blow not to my knee but to my soul. It struck at all I valued, all I had worked to be. They said it was business. I was damaged goods. The prospect of recovery was uncertain, and the team would not wait. So, suddenly, it was over. I left at once.

Rikki and I sat in the house in Leesburg, all 5,000 square feet of it. Good thing we had only rented and not purchased it. With the loss of my job, it had to go. We would move to a two-bedroom apartment in Richmond. It felt like moving with only one duffle bag again. I wasn't in a place where I could hear the lesson, but it is striking now. We don't need all of the stuff we accumulate. All we really need is already inside us, in abundance.

Hurt and angry, I refused to accept that this was the last word on me and my career. I began phoning and researching. Who could treat my knee, who could get me ready to play as soon as possible? I began to go off-script, writing my own playbook for a challenge I never imagined. I had always presumed the durability of my body. Someone, somewhere would figure out what was needed to heal. I still failed to grasp that healing involved more than the knee.

A friend and Arizona teammate, Larry Fitzgerald, connected me to Dr. Josh Sandell, a chiropractor and physical therapist in the Minneapolis area. Soon I went there. Even before I was released by Washington, it sounded like he might have an answer. It would be one of the first of hundreds of trips crossing the country over the next few years. Doctors, clinics, gyms, therapies, programs. Then medications and treatments by the score. It feels like I did it all. Dozens of stops, many more than once. Going for stem cell, ozone, collagen, PRP, and other rare treatments. Even looking into Regenokine, which Kobe Bryant supposedly tried. Life became a cascading series of efforts to heal the knee, by one means or another.

Early on, as I frantically tried to heal, Dr. Josh became a frequent stop. After an initial, thorough examination, lasting hours and including an MRI, he wondered aloud if the knee was infected. I returned to Pensacola and the surgeon who had performed the surgery. He dismissed the idea of an infection. Instead, he performed a second surgery, declaring that scar tissue had been removed and the knee now would be fine with more rehab. Encouraged I moved ahead with the rehab and more conditioning.

The knee had to be fine. It just had to. NFL teams were phoning. It was not widely known why Washington had cut me.

I was seen as a starting running back who was at the peak of his career. But things were not fine. No amount of rehab and training made the knee fine. It remained sore and swollen. There was a problem that was getting worse, not better, whether the NFL teams were interested or not.

The problem was not just in the left knee. I was losing myself. I was ceasing to be the person I intended to be, with no clear way back. Recovery was becoming more than healing the knee. It meant finding myself, perhaps for the first time. Who was I beyond football? That was a frightening question I could not yet face.

Desperate to hold onto the image of the starting NFL running back, to imagine that more football recognition lay ahead, I did things I never would have done before the injury. I began hanging out in nightclubs and other places where someone, including women, might recognize me. I wanted to be seen, to be known and admired. I would give some autographs, tell some stories, and get a few free drinks. I cheapened who I was and what I had accomplished. But it became like a drug I needed to sustain the image of who I was.

I have never liked to drink. If I am honest, I would readily say that I have never liked the taste of alcoholic beverages of any kind. I tell my kids that now. But I was caught up in an image to which I tried to cling. The image of the athlete, the running back, the celebrity. Looking back it was all so superficial.

The reality was that life as I wanted it was slipping away. I tried to cling to superficial bits of it. But that did not work, and my mood only became worse. There was no hiding, no escape. A swollen, throbbing left knee interrupted every flight of fantasy.

Still, I refused to deal. I thought I was dealing with more exercises, more therapies, more travel to one clinic or another.

But I wasn't dealing with what was deeper than the knee. The only constant now was Rikki, my wife. Even now, I marvel at her patience and understanding.

Early on, we started a journal together. We prayed together. We were both in, full commitment. She was on board. She even let go of some career opportunities. She could have gone places. Instead, she put her emphasis on our marriage and healing the knee. Looking back, she was and is incredible.

Now, Rikki describes just how difficult things became. "Tim became very shaken when football was in doubt. He was stubborn in his approach to recovery. At first, he would not take pain medication. He wanted to heal naturally. But the doctors and I all told him that he could not do rehab if he was in severe pain. So, he looked for over-the-counter medication. He wanted to take the least possible amount of pain medication and to do the maximum amount of rehab."

But, as there was no sign of healing, I distanced myself from her, and from everyone else. Rikki and I became like ships passing silently in the night. I wasn't there for her emotionally. I could only do what I was accustomed to doing. Work and more work. Doing it sullenly was no solution and only made everything worse, including the knee. But, for the time being, I could not see what was going on; I could not see the big picture.

Then teams stopped calling. Still, I worked, now more privately than ever. I tried everything that came to mind. I even brought in the team of therapists I had assembled while in Phoenix. They did their best. Briefly, the knee felt better. Yet it would not heal. It remained sore and swollen. The pain, now spread through my life, would not go away.

By then more than a year had passed. Nothing was working. Even worse, medical insurance was gone and the money was drying up. There was no income and the savings account was in free fall. Just like my life. Plunging downward. From anxious yet focused, I had gone to sullen and withdrawn. The next stage was angry and almost totally internalized. It was more obvious than ever that my identity and my life were in tatters. There was no direction other than the pursuit of the next specialist and more expensive therapy requiring airfares and hotel bills.

Dr. Josh in Minneapolis began to offer rare support. He sensed that the problem was more than the knee. He began to treat me without charge and offered me a place to stay in his home. He was determined to get the knee, and my life, healed. He listened, a rare quality in all of the medical people I consulted. Most had answers without really hearing the questions. Every time Dr. Josh listened and, often, he quietly suggested that an infection was to blame. But that idea had been excluded and I was not ready to consider it. I was plunging headlong into more travel and more evaluations, more treatments, and more exercise. More, more, more. Maybe what I really needed was to stop and to listen.

At the time, this frantic pursuit was what I needed to do. It was the style I had cultivated, of reaching and over-reaching. I would outwork everyone. That was the way to results. Only this work ethic was not working. It had become the worst approach I could have chosen. It threatened to wreck my relationships. Already there was damage needing repair well beyond the knee. My soul had scar tissue. I was losing sight of what was worthwhile, what should have been primary.

I would have to discover, as never before, how to listen as well as to act, and, especially, how to gauge the impact of my actions on those around me. It was as if I was a kid again, learning to dream, only now dreaming of being whole. It was a journey into faith, more than memorizing Bible passages and assuming I knew the answers. It meant learning to question vigorously. Learning how to find, learning how to search, learning how to pause and take stock. The lessons would pile up. My life was on the line, as I was beginning to understand.

I had felt abandoned by God. I wondered, "why me?" What had I done other than work hard and try to provide for my family? I examined my life over and over, still not getting any clarity. I would learn that faith is not a rabbit's foot, not protection from life's harsh realities. I had given money to the church, but also felt abandoned by them. What did it all mean? Hard work and dedication and loyalty are supposed to lead to reward. That stream had dried up, just like my checkbook. Where was God? Where was the way out?

Things were coming to a head. I would have to face various realities, some that went beyond the football field. On one of my visits to Dr. Josh, he wanted to take me to his favorite steak house. I agreed because he was supporting me. But it did not feel right. I did not know at first, but it did not have a good feel.

Once we reached the restaurant, in Maple Grove, Minnesota, I immediately realized there was no one there who looked like me. Meaning, I was the only African-American person in this suburban place. Still, I settled in for a quiet meal with a friend and supporter. Then, perhaps five minutes into the meal, the waitress stopped, not to ask how we were enjoying the food. Nervously, she told me that two men outside wanted to see me. This was odd. Perhaps they wanted autographs or wanted to talk football. I decided to enjoy a few more bites and stroll outside to see who was there.

Then the restaurant's manager came over, even more nervous and insistent. Now there were three men outside and they were police. I had to go outside immediately. Setting down my fork, and my napkin, I quietly walked outside wondering what in the world this was about. I was beginning to get hot, to feel anger. Fortunately, Josh came along. As I reached the police, I checked Josh's face. It was red, radiating embarrassment. It was doubly fortunate that I began to assume this was a prank he had designed. I smiled and even laughed, thinking I had caught on. No one else laughed.

It was no joke. Sternly one of the police announced that someone in the restaurant thought I looked like a picture they had seen on a wanted poster, of a fugitive accused of serious crimes. I had to produce an ID and wait, now becoming angry again. Then, maybe miraculously, one of the police officers connected the dots. He played fantasy football and actually had chosen me as a player on his fantasy team. My ID was returned, and the police apologized. But the meal to which Josh and I returned did not taste the same.

I had shared with Josh what it feels like to be Black in America. He seemed to understand. I did not doubt his sincerity. But my experience had been an abstraction to him, until that night at the steakhouse in Maple Grove. He saw how easily suspicion can fall on African-American men in particular. I have thought about that incident as tensions and discussions have grown around the police department in Minneapolis. But it is every city. There is an injury, a chronic infection, that needs healing. Gradually I was seeing beyond myself and simply getting back to the NFL. My life was larger. The world's realities were larger. There was much to be faced, in the knee and well beyond it.

After all the doctor visits and treatments, something still wasn't right. I had gone to clinics and offices in Florida, Minnesota, Virginia, California, Arizona, and New York. Hundreds of thousands of dollars had been spent yet there were no answers. Was this comeback just not meant to be? Were there realities too large to overcome? Why was I chasing this idea that I could return to football after being told "no" by those who were considered to be among the best in their fields?

How long do you hold onto something? To a dream, or a relationship, or an idea? How does one know when it is over, when it is time to move on to something else? I had so many questions and so few answers. I had made a few friends but nothing conclusive had surfaced to resolve the condition of my knee or to heal my life. Where could I turn now?

I had gone from being a world-class athlete, one who had ascended to the top of the competition at every level to someone who could not walk up and down stairs without pain. I had prided myself on being in the best physical condition and on overcoming any challenge. "What you can control in sports are your condition and your attitude," my dad always told me. I took that advice to heart. I did not worry if I was third on the depth chart, if a coach liked me, or if I was as talented as my peers. I still could control how hard I worked and how I viewed myself.

I recalled days in high school, waking up early in the morning to jog to school or begin an early workout. I would complete the workout and then jog home. In college, I would find out what workout routine was planned for the day, then go to the track early in the morning and do it, returning later in the day to complete it again with my teammates. Early in my NFL career, a veteran player told me I was "working too hard." That became a mark of pride. My dad was right. Being in the best physical shape gave me an inner confidence and peace. I knew I had done all I could do, and I counted on that serving me well.

I knew I was prepared. I trusted the outcome would be in my favor, sooner or later.

Those times seemed like distant memories. Three years of pain and uncertainty felt like a decade. I was no longer able to run, jump, and challenge my body. Exercise had brought me confidence and had shaped my body. It also shaped and reinforced my identity. It had also been an outlet when there was frustration to release. Now, there was no way to let go of the greatest stress ever, of the pain, physical and spiritual, that hung over me every day. I struggled to find alternative outlets. But, for three years, the answer I sought had eluded me. There were no answers to what was going on in the knee. As the crisis dragged on, I was losing myself.

One day as I searched for answers, I received a phone call from my former Arizona teammate, Beanie Wells. He asked how the knee was doing and I told him I was still not there. Beanie was also going through knee rehab. He told me about a doctor in Houston who had helped him. I was reluctant. This was good encouragement from a friend, but yet another doctor? I had been to enough doctors to last a lifetime. Beanie assured me the doctor was good and sent along his contact information. I sent him a text and he responded shortly. He wanted to speak with me to discuss the situation.

Had I lost my mind? Was I just chasing a fantasy? I needed to do something I had not done enough of in recent months: talk to Rikki. We were starting to build back our marriage. Talking to her now was doubly important. So, we discussed, and we prayed to God for guidance. I knew I needed more surgery, but what if this didn't fix anything? Would this make my chances of returning even worse? How realistic is it to think a team would sign a player who had been out for three years and had multiple surgeries? Especially a running back with a bad knee. With young talent coming in every year, why would a team want damaged goods?

I told Rikki I was not sure what to do. I considered calling people for advice and actually picked up the phone, then set it down. Paralysis by analysis. As I often did, I did a mental scan of past experiences, trying to identify a time when I had faced a similar challenge. But nothing like this surfaced. I realized that I no longer trusted myself to make a thoughtful choice.

It was ironic. Three years before, on the football field, I made decisions in less than three seconds while scrutinized by coaches, players, and tens of thousands of fans. Eleven opponents were after me and I would have to decide and decide again, usually on instinct. But that instinct seemed gone, and I was stuck. The reality was that this involved more than the purpose of playing football and more than the determination to be in top condition. This was new territory—after I had been disappointed so many times as I dragged my knee across the country.

Rikki was there, all in. She wanted me to be happy. She wanted me to be at peace, to find answers, about football and more. She wanted me to finish what I had started and to walk away with no regrets. It was reassuring. She wanted what I wanted.

OK, so we are on the same page. Now what? Forget money or lack of resources. Flying to Houston for evaluation and likely surgery seemed to be the best step. At least there might be some resolution. With the decision made, there was a sense of fresh air. I was not out of the woods. I needed to find much more of myself. But this was a much-needed step. And we had taken it together. Maybe there was a way out of the woods. We had to follow the path together. Already I felt better.

Chapter Eleven

IN A VULNERABLE PLACE

Practical details always intrude. Rikki and I had talked it through. I would go to Houston for an evaluation. We were emotionally ready. Now we just needed to get there. Money was low. I had spent a lot of money on experimental treatments. This doctor and this place needed to work. He was reassuring. So, I went to Houston.

When I finally got there and met with the doctor, I felt a peace I had not felt with most of the others. By then, three years into this strange journey, there had been dozens of medical professionals. This one seemed to listen and genuinely wanted to help. He did not promise to fix everything but assured me he would do his best. If he could not, he would find someone who could. He did not seem concerned. There were x-rays and tests and his own examination. Nothing seemed surprising. He proceeded with an injection. There were instructions to stay off the leg for a few days and then I should be ready to go. So, back to Richmond where we lived.

As promised, a few days later, most of the pain was gone and swelling was down. But the knee was not 100 percent. I wondered if this was the best it would ever feel. It was a tiresome question. When you've experienced the best, it is difficult to think that you must settle for something less. I reasoned with myself. Give it a few more days. But that didn't work. So, I reasoned again. I could play with this level of pain. Then it got steadily worse. After two weeks, the pain and swelling were back. I contacted the doctor and returned to Houston for more treatment.

Then the pain and swelling returned one week after treatment. I again contacted the doctor. He sounded appalled and my anxiety rose. He had been composed and confident in the beginning. Now he communicated uncertainty. I flew to Houston for a third time, and fortunately, this doctor was as good as his word. He was determined to find the answer. He was so concerned that he referred me to Dr. David Lintner.

I phoned Dr. Lintner and left a voicemail. I had learned that he was team doctor for several of Houston's professional sports teams. When he returned the call, Dr. Lintner had already spoken with the previous doctor. "It sounds like something is going on in that knee," he said. This was not the most encouraging start. It got worse. "The only way to figure out what is really going on is to perform surgery to explore." Yea, right, more surgery. Which already seemed like a dead end. Please, no more surgery. Wasn't there another way?

Back in Richmond, I lay on the bed staring at the wall. "What do you want to do?" Rikki asked. We prayed. "God, give us guidance." So many thoughts popped up. How do I know if we're making the right decision? I knew I needed surgery but what if this didn't fix anything? Would this make the chances of returning to the NFL worse, not better? How realistic is it to think a team would be interested in a guy who had become almost three years removed from playing with multiple surgeries in between? Worse, how interested would they be in a running back with a bum knee? The average NFL career is only three years. Young talent comes in every year. There are a lot of hungry guys wanting to play. What makes damaged goods more appealing?

Thoughts became a flood of feelings and anxiety. "I'm not sure what to do," I told Rikki. "But I can't make a decision on the basis of fear." My mind raced through memories of past experiences trying to locate a time when I faced a similar challenge. There had been many, but none like this. None like this ongoing, unclear, unresolved knee problem. I didn't know what to do, so I picked up the phone and began scrolling. Who could I call for advice? Then I set the phone down. I had spent nearly three years hearing various opinions, trying to follow various forms of advice. The more opinions came in, the more uncertain the situation became. Paralysis by analysis. How did this happen? The search for answers had become a confusion of approaches, people, and programs. They had all been so confident. Now I was not confident at all. I realized I no longer trusted myself to make the right choice. That seemed to be the only outcome of this struggle. I felt vulnerable as never before.

How had I reached such a place? For most of my life there had been a goal and intense focus on it. How could this focus, this certainty, have disappeared? I had gone toe to toe with anyone who had challenged my goal of playing professional football. Hadn't I sacrificed hours and hours to develop the skills required on and off the field? There had been support from family and friends. But my journey, my goal, was central. On any question, the decision-making process was simple: how does this impact the goal of being on the football field? It was just that simple. Each decision and each relationship was considered in relation to the goal. It was very efficient. It produced confidence. It made sense. For a long time, it worked. Then it stopped working.

So, how did I get to the point where I no longer trusted myself to make decisions? I wondered about this intently, silently, staring at the ceiling. Enough is enough. But where to turn? Where to go? "What do you want?" I finally asked Rikki. "I want you to be happy," she quickly replied. "OK, thanks, but what do you want to happen in this situation?" I answered a question with a question. That's where this process had led. "Well, I want you to find answers. I want you to be at peace and not stressed out. I want you to finish what's in your heart to do—if that's to continue in football or not. I don't want you to have any regrets. I just want us to make a decision and to move forward." It was a remarkable response. It was a gift of love.

I listened. What she wanted was exactly what I wanted. She had said it well. I was tired of being afraid. I did not want regrets and mostly I wanted to heal and return to football. We were on the same page. So, what is the best decision we can make? Forget money or lack of resources. At least for the moment. First, figure out what will be best. We agreed that flying back to Houston and having the surgery was the right decision. Then there would be answers. At least we would know more about what is going on. Decision made. There was the feeling of being in fresh air. Fear of the wrong decision can paralyze. At least we were not stuck. We had the beginning of a plan. Still, more answers were needed. But now there was a plan.

But how would we get there? I phoned the doctor who had referred us to Dr. Lintner. He sounded pleased to hear our decision. "That's a good choice," he said. "I just want you to find the answers you are needing," he added. Wow, I thought, that's exactly what Rikki said. It was amazing that as soon as a decision was made, support from people around me was apparent. The doctor agreed to help with transportation to and from Houston, and lodging when we were there. That was big. I hung up and told Rikki.

She smiled. "OK, then," she added, "How will we eat while we are there?" I logged onto my bank account hoping that miraculously the balance would have improved. But there was still $5 to our name. The monthly bills had come off, leaving us $5 and nothing more. I instantly felt shame and embarrassment. What would people think? An NFL star with a measly $5 in his bank account. How could that happen?

I had become a statistic I had fought my whole life to avoid. Growing up I heard about all sorts of grim statistics for African-American males. I was determined this would not be me. I would not spend a day in prison. I would graduate from college. I would play in the NFL and I would retire with millions in the bank. I had successfully checked off three of those items on the list. So how did I end up with $5 to my name? I had not purchased expensive cars. I did not buy a big house. I rented a small townhouse. I did not buy jewelry. I felt like I had avoided the major pitfalls. I had tried to do everything right. Yet her I was. How did this happen?

No time for pity. Decisions had been made. Now we had to return to Houston. As I stared at the phone and the bank account, hoping for something to change, Rikki asked how much money was in the bank. I did not want to lie to her but could not bring myself to tell the truth. "We will figure it out." That was all I could say. She could tell things were not good, but she did not press the issue. We were living on the top floor of my godparents' house in Richmond. I texted Aleta, my godmother, and told her of the decision to get surgery. I added that we would be flying back to Houston in the next day or two. "I pray that you get the answers you are looking for and are able to put this behind you," she replied. Another wow moment. Just like what Rikki and the doctor had said. I always felt better after talking to Aleta. Even more so now.

Rikki and I packed our bags and tried to get a decent night's sleep. That night I felt peace. I had no clue what the doctor would find, I still did not have money, nor did I know how I would take care of a pregnant wife. By now, Rikki was carrying our first child. But for the first time in a long time, we had made a decision together. A decision without fear. I knew I had made the best choice for us. My life's script was being rewritten, bit by bit. Life was going to be different.

The next day, as we headed out the door to the airport, Aleta gave me a hug and handed me an envelope. I opened it and saw $50. How did she know? Was this an answered prayer? I hugged her, thanked her, and walked out the door. As I drove to the Richmond airport, I simply said, "Thank you, God." Prayer had been answered, again. The doctor, the transportation, and now this gift. I still did not have the full picture, but these small, answered prayers gave me confidence to move ahead. Answers to the big questions must be close.

An important answer surfaced quickly. Upon opening up the knee, Dr. Lintner found the problem. ACL surgery typically involves a pin to hold the transferred ligament in place. Often the pin used is synthetic. It is designed to dissolve as healing proceeds. In a few cases, the pin does not dissolve. It can be rejected by the body's immune system as a foreign object. It can also become infected. In a few instances, the infection can spread beyond the knee into the body.

I proved to have an unusual case. The area around the pin had become infected. Pain and swelling in the knee were evidence of infection that had resisted detection until Dr. Lintner took a look. Somewhat surprising, the infection had been confined to the area of the pin. There was no spread of the infection beyond the knee. The spread of infection could require amputation of some or all of the leg. Somehow that would not be my fate.

What to do next? The infection cleaned out, I moved full speed ahead on rehabilitation and recovery. Perhaps there was still a way back. The dream had faded. Now it burst forth again. But life would have to be different. There were signs that it was.

Through Karlos Dansby, a friend, and former teammate, I learned of Dr. Leon Mellman in Florida. I sent blood samples to him and he did a comprehensive analysis. His specialty is diet, eating the right foods to maximize body performance. Soon I was engaged. Bison, almond oil, blueberries became the staples. He was meticulous, easily reached, responsive to all questions. The diet proved transformative.

My body was returning. The knee felt good. I was working out and letting it be known that I was ready to come back. It was early 2014. There was time to get ready. Sure enough, two teams, Miami and Cleveland, discussed tryouts. I scheduled a workout with Cleveland. Hope and anticipation returned, like old friends. Kyle Shanahan, who had been my offensive coordinator at Washington, now was at Cleveland. He had told me the game was on my shoulders, moments before the injury. Perhaps I could pick up where I left off.

It was not to be. Days before the Cleveland workout, I awoke one morning to find the knee, the same knee, swollen and painful. Hugely painful. I soon was speaking to Dr. Mellman in Florida. He told me not to waste time. Go to the emergency room nearest you. Rikki had to help me walk. It was a difficult time for her. She was still pregnant, our first child almost due. Plus, her mother, dying of cancer, had moved in. Now, I could not walk to the car without assistance. Had all of this work been for naught?

The infection had returned. That could be clearly established. Another surgery was needed, immediately. The return of infection brought back all the concerns about wider infection and loss of the limb. Again, I dodged a bullet. Again, the infection was confined and again it could be cleaned out.

Back to work on all fronts. An important realization crept over me. I was awakening to the fact that I had not been there for Rikki. She had certainly been there for me. She had even dropped her career. She had invested emotionally in my pursuits, my injury, my efforts to find new balance. For too long I had stayed angry, disconnected. Somehow, we made it through, mainly because of her. It was time to be part of our marriage, to be emotionally engaged myself.

That was not easy though it became necessary. I felt punished by God. I faced the reality that faith is not a lucky charm that steers us away from harm. Wasn't Jesus supposed to protect me? Wasn't Jesus supposed to reward me if I did all the right things? As I soared up to the NFL, I thought that. After that bitter day in Charlotte, I did not know what I thought, what I believed.

New realizations were taking hold. Faith is about guidance, not protection, about finding the pathway on life's difficult journey. Part of faith is finding fresh, healthy connections to one another. I began to seek that with Rikki, on a new basis. New appreciation of life surfaced. Aleta Richards understands and says it well. "I kept trying to tell Tim that he has so many skills. I kept asking him what was Plan B? For a long time, even thinking about Plan B meant admitting failure. But gradually, slowly, he began to talk about new possibilities."

I went with my wife to a family gathering in North Carolina. Clearly, she was surprised. I didn't simply say I would go I actually went. And was glad that I did. Meanwhile, never closing the door to football, I began working at a commercial real estate firm in Richmond. It was income and taking this job signaled that my sense of the future was expanding. Still, the mention of football could never be casual. One day, a co-worker made a surprising offer. "Hey Tim," the new friend said. "I have an extra ticket for the Monday night game, Redskins and Seahawks. Do you want to go?"

My immediate thought was "Heck no." Why would I want to watch someone else play when I should be playing? On top of that, Washington. The same team that lied to my face and released me. My reply was visceral: No thanks, I'll pass. But those words never left my head.

"When do you need to know?" I wondered aloud. "Tomorrow," he said. "I just do not want to waste the ticket. No pressure. I just figured you may want to go."

As I left the office that afternoon, I wondered: Why should I go? Doesn't he know what it feels like to be forced to watch someone else do what you love? I was not ready to become a "fan." I wanted to play. I refused to go to receptions for "retired" athletes. I would not check a box on a form that said "injury." I believe that when you want something, all actions and thoughts should align with what you believe. This mindset served me well growing up. As a young kid, you absorb information and try to grasp what it all means. Cutting off opinions and people that do not align with your beliefs can simplify life. But as I got older, I noticed myself becoming more shut off to people, to new ideas and opportunities. Knowing when certain instincts no longer serve you is a gift that comes with wisdom and time. I began to notice the motivation behind my decisions and to ask if I made decisions based on pride. Pride was dangerous. I couldn't see opportunity when I held onto pride.

Was this an opportunity? Would going to this game take me a step closer to the NFL? Maybe it could put me in an environment where the dream comes alive again. It's Washington, the last team who saw something in me. I had become healthy again, yet teams did not believe it. All they knew was I had been out for three years and had multiple surgeries. If I could get the Redskins team docs to evaluate me and affirm that I was healthy, maybe it would go a long way with the rest of the teams. The doctor who performed my surgery would be at the game. He attended all home games. He had influence across the league. That's it! I would reach out to him and have him evaluate me at halftime. I started to get excited.

Until you embrace uncomfortable situations, you are unable to see opportunity. Just as I started to send a text confirming I would go, I still hesitated. Wait, I thought. You're going to go to the game as a fan and somehow manage to get down to the locker room for a team doc to see you? It's been three years. They won't know you. You will look desperate. But it was too late. I saw the opportunity, and at this point, the thought of getting what I wanted was worth the thought of embarrassment. I sent my co-worker a text, "I'm in", then quickly sent the team doc a text letting him know I would be at the game and would

like to see him. He immediately responded, "Absolutely." Now
the idea did not seem so crazy.

As we drove to the stadium, I wondered how I would get
down to the locker room. I tried to entertain conversation about
who had the better team, who did I think would win. But I was
not a fan. I knew why I was there. A part of me felt bad. Like I
was using my co-worker to get something I wanted. But he had
asked me to go. I continued with small talk and tried to seem
excited about watching the game. By the time we arrived, I was
nervous. There still was no plan. The first quarter went by; I
watched but was not paying attention. As halftime approached,
still no plan that made sense. Finally, I thought, *it's now or
never*. I came here to see a doc and I'm not leaving until I do.
I texted the doc, "I am here and I'm coming to see you." He
did not ask how I was getting to him, or where I was. For all
he knew, there was no way I could get down there. I politely
excused myself from my colleague and went to find my way.

My heart was racing. Where was the locker room? I had
never been in the stands. Just a few years ago I was being
escorted into the locker room by security and now I'm in the
nosebleed section trying to find my way to it. It brought humil-
ity about how quickly things can change. I looked around and
asked a volunteer for directions and he reluctantly pointed to
his right, confused as to why I would ask this question. His
direction led me to the elevators. Again, I had to ask for directions. I changed my tactic to hide my intention. Another volunteer stopped the elevator at one level and explained that I would
have to exit and get on another elevator to go down to the base-
ment level. Now the adrenaline began to rush. I was amazed
at the support I received along the way. Not one question as to
why I wanted to know. Were these people crazy? I could have

been anyone! They must have sensed that I was politely determined. I knew what I wanted and would get there by any means necessary. I believe when people recognize this type of passion it draws them to either help or get out of the way.

I arrived at the VIP elevator. Unlike the first two, this elevator was guarded. Security people were there, men with walkie-talkies. I stood back to watch the demeanor of those who approached it. Men and women with business suits. They walked confidently to the elevator nodded and walked on. I took mental notes, reminded myself of my purpose, and confidently proceeded to do the same thing. I nodded at the security guard and proceeded to walk on the elevator. "Which floor?" He asked. "Home team locker room," I responded. Not the right answer. I drew a red flag. "What department are you with?" "Veterans," I said instinctively. "I am an alumni player and I am going to meet with the team doctor." "Do you have credentials?" he asked? "Not on me," I replied. "I was not told that I would need them." My mind raced to respond with confidence. I stated my name, hoping that would ring a bell. He replied, "Who?"

Then he called his colleague and described the situation. Fortunately, the other security guard recognized me. "I'm a big fan. What are you doing here? Why did they not give you credentials?" I shrugged. My demeanor had changed. I was no longer a random stranger. My confidence grew. "Look, I just need to see the doc. Can you call down to the locker room, he is expecting me." As he called, I thought, less than thirty minutes ago I was nervous and without a plan. I was amazed at how far determination had gotten me. It felt good. It had been a long time since I experienced this kind of confidence.

After a few calls, he opened the elevator and said I could not get in contact with the doctor but make sure they give you credentials when you get there. I assured him I would and walked onto the elevator. When I arrived at the locker room, the players were walking past headed back to the field. I recognized a few, exchanged handshakes, but was not interested in conversation. They were focused, as was I. "Where is the doc," I asked? Someone pointed.

"You made it," he said, surprised that I had gotten down there. It was as if he was not expecting me. "How are you feeling?" he asked. "I'm fine. I just need you to examine my knee." He twisted, turned, checked for swelling and pain. None. He stepped back looked at me in amazement and said, "Looks good to me. I would pass you on a physical." That's it! All of this effort for a brief evaluation. I proceeded. "Doc, it would go a long way if you sent out a letter to teams saying that you evaluated me and I was healthy and cleared of any injury." He shook my hand and assured me he would. I thanked him and walked out. "Hey Tim," he said, looking back. "I guess it was an infection after all." No kidding!

Chapter Twelve

SEE ME FOR WHO I AM

I began to emerge from the shell I had built around myself. The injury followed by inconclusive efforts to learn what prevented healing had become a shell of its own. I was intently focused on getting to the bottom of the knee's swelling and pain so I could return to the NFL. But long before the injury there had been a shell. Construction began when I was a child. Like much in life, my personal shell had its strengths and limitations. With the injury, and the struggles it triggered, there was much to face about myself and the life I had built.

By focusing intently on football, I had developed qualities that would serve anyone well: above all, determination and purpose. I had athletic ability and I had fine-tuned it to a high degree. I became a team leader wherever I played, someone who could rally his teammates. I knew what hard work it took to pursue a goal. I meant to inspire that dedication in others. I had built a reputation as a successful athlete and a person of character and values.

However, life had been almost exclusively football. Those to whom I became close accepted that football would define me. Rikki, especially, had been incredibly understanding. A few others who were close, such as Aleta and Bob, my godparents, accepted my focus. Other friendships mostly had arisen through athletics. That was the common ground. It was a tightly defined life with a narrow focus. Success on the football field demanded no less. So long as it worked, it was great. It was virtually life itself.

After that game in Charlotte, and the injury that resisted all efforts to resolve it, I withdrew and often was sullen. As I've described, my old approach of working harder and focusing more narrowly on what needed attention did not solve the problem, the largest problem I had ever faced. That frustration in itself challenged who I was, how I had made a career, where I had decided to go in life. My knee did not truly begin to heal until the stubborn, hidden infection was discovered nearly three years after the original injury. But my life needed to do more than heal. I needed to emerge for the first time. The singular focus that had defined me also brought blinders. Now they began to come off. My life was forced to widen. I was compelled to see things differently.

A prime instance came in 2013 as I continued rehab. Swimming had become part of my workouts. I had relied on swimming after I broke my foot in high school. Workouts in the pool are tough. This experience came to mind and I started to swim regularly.

I was able to return to Arizona for workouts and went to a particular gym, regularly swimming then spending time in the hot tub. One day I struck up a conversation with a man named Jack Ross. It's odd how some friendships arise. A surprising synchronicity can appear, if only we pay attention to it. At one time, I might not have noticed. It still seems odd. My mother-in-law had given me a book by Magic Johnson about his own recovery. In the book he noted an interest in commercial real estate. To my surprise, I found this intriguing. Not long before, I would have shrugged it off as unrelated to my pursuits. Still, I did not know anyone in the field, so how would I ever explore commercial real estate?

How odd could it be that Jack Ross, with whom I began to build a friendship at the gym in Phoenix, was in commercial real estate?! He and I began to have serious conversation. He began to describe his work. Before long, I would find an opportunity at a firm in Richmond. Meanwhile, something more important was happening. I built trust in someone who would have been a casual friend at best before my life took an unexpected turn.

I held back at first. I did not even mention football initially. Jack soon learned of my career and my story. Then I felt embarrassed and vulnerable. Without football, who was I? I was still emerging from the shell. Answers were unfolding just as answers to the knee's situation were appearing. Jack was very helpful. I swallowed my pride and spoke honestly. I admitted that I needed guidance. It was tough. I was struggling. Jack stepped up in various ways, especially as a mentor and friend. He became someone I could trust for reliable advice. He gave support in various ways as I turned the biggest corner in life I had ever faced. Football had been my only option. I was discovering that there could be other options and other people. And, that I had to become a different person. It was difficult, but it was happening. Tim was emerging.

"There are times when you need to let go and move on," Aleta observes. "Change is not failure. And there are many things you never have to give up, such as loved ones and your personal values."

More change would unfold. For the time being, I was not done with football. Even as life opened up, as I connected with other people and with myself, I had to give it another try. So, I worked out intently, daily, and was in good shape. By the fall of 2014, the knee had healed and there was fresh hope a team would call.

Emotionally I still could not watch a full game. But I knew everything that was happening across the league. Who got signed, traded, or injured. Who the top performers were for the week. Every Sunday evening, I checked every highlight of every game. I tried to anticipate what teams may need a running back. I phoned my agent frequently, always asking the same question: "Has anyone called," only to hear the same response, "No, not yet." I called though I already knew the answer. Your agent must be aware of every football transaction that occurs each week. The agent should notify you when there are opportunities while encouraging teams to be interested in you. A good agent knows the opportunities before you do as a player. If they are not calling you, it means either you need a new agent, or you need a new career path.

One day, I sat in my office working commercial real estate, trying to adjust to life behind a desk. I struggled. My eyes wouldn't stay open, even after eight hours of sleep the night before. It was hard to focus. I had posted motivational screen savers and quotes around my office, but they were not working. I had an interest in learning commercial real estate. But there was unfinished business on the gridiron. That's where energy and attention were flowing.

Then the phone rang. It was my agent, Eugene Parker. I sat up straight in my chair. "Tim, it's Eugene. The Redskins want to bring you in for a workout." Before he could finish my heart raced even as I tried to be calm. "Ok cool, tell me when," I stammered. "The workout is tomorrow. You will do a physical and on field workout. I don't want to promise you anything. They are bringing in a bunch of guys and don't plan on signing anyone. They just want to see where you are physically." Of all he said, I heard only that there was an opportunity, which was all I ever wanted. Who cared about the odds or how many other people were going for the job? Give me an opportunity any day and I'll show what I can do. I thanked him for the call, assured him I was ready, and hung up.

I sat back in my chair and took a deep breath. I'm back. I said a quick prayer, "Thank you God, I'm ready." Then I called Rikki. For the first time in a long time, I smiled. All of the sleepless nights, tossing and turning. All of the surgeries. Waking up early before work to train for two hours was worth it. I was ready mentally and physically. In the NFL, you're either ready or you're not. You step up and deliver when it's your time or they move on to someone else. I knew this as I trained each morning. I would close my eyes before reps and imagine being in the huddle, game on the line, and they call my number. My training intensity was game simulated. When opportunities come, you must be prepared, and I was.

Quickly, I went home to pack and be sure I had everything: cleats, compression pants, lacrosse ball for warmup and cool down, essential oils, supplements. All there. Time to drive to Washington. I said one last prayer with Rikki and the kids. She looked at me smiling. "You're going to do great. I'm proud of you." I smiled, hugged her and kissed her. I tried to stay composed. Her words brought out every emotion in me. Coming from Rikki they carried great weight. She went through the ups and downs and witnessed how this journey brought out the worst and the best of me. To have the respect of the ones closest to me and to make them proud had become my feeling of success.

I barely slept the night before the workout. So many thoughts raced through my mind. I told myself, try to maintain focus and stick to the routine. This isn't the time to switch things up. In big moments you don't invent new things, your trust your preparation. Trust what you know. I went through my process, warm Epsom salt bath mixed with essential oils, followed by a nighttime stretch routine, feet elevated up the wall, eyes closed, visualizing the success of the next day. I said my prayers, sent Rikki one last text and fell asleep.

I don't know why I was surprised the next morning to see about a dozen other running backs prepared to workout. I always embraced competition. Did I think I would be the only one? I sized them up: some veterans, some young guys and others who had never played an NFL snap. I convinced myself that no one had worked harder to get there. No one wanted this as badly as I did. I shook hands and gave head nods, but I was uninterested in speaking. I only wanted to hit the field. As I saw other guys embracing each other, laughing, part of me envied them. I admired those who appeared focused while enjoying the moment. I would watch guys form connections and bonds bigger than the game itself. They built respect for each other. I was never one to make a lot of friends within football. The game brought out a focus, passion and drive for me. I was only interested in winning and being the best I could be. That could bring isolation. Looking back, I was fortunate to have a few friendships. I'm not sure if I would have done it differently,

I just noticed the difference in approach. I was seeing much I never saw before.

After initial physicals and interviews, it was time to hit the field. I laced up my cleats and began to warm up. My body felt strong, my adrenaline was beginning to rush. Don't overdo it Tim, I kept telling myself. Stick to the process, trust the routine. Everyone had their own routine and rhythm. You could see which guys had no clue. Unprepared, they watched, trying to improvise, imitating the actions of others with no real understanding. Then the coaches walked in and it was time to go.

As they called out the drills, I jumped to the front of the line. A fist to the heart, a kiss of two fingers, a point to the sky, "Thank you, God." I went through the first drill and felt something fall off my wrist. I ran back to retrieve it. It was the hospital band from when my son was born. Chills ran through my body. I believe in watching the signs of life. I had promised that I would not take off that band until I signed an NFL contract. It was when I was fresh from more surgery, navigating between Rikki's birthing room to my own room as I received antibiotics to treat the infection in my knee. My mother-in-law fought for her life as I fought for my career and my wife fought for the birth of our first child all at the same time. As I held my son in the hospital, I made a promise: "You will see me play football, son. I won't give up. I promise." At every step of this journey, I asked God to give me a sign that I was on the right path. This was a sign. I picked up the band, smiled and stuffed it in my compression tights. My focus intensified.

I was happy when I finished the workout. I saw some guys hunched over, others with their heads down wishing they could have one drill back. Not me. I had done my best. I was prepared and I gave it everything. I felt quick, strong, explosive. I was back. In my mind it wasn't even close. I could see the look on the faces of scouts and coaches. They were impressed. I prepared myself to sign a contract and finish what I started three years earlier.

After showering and getting dressed I met with the head scout. He had a serious look on his face. "Awesome workout TH. You look strong, healthy." *Yeah, I know, get to the good part,* I think. "Your workout was by far the best out of anyone here, good enough for us to sign you. We should sign you, but we won't now. Our doctors are hesitant with your injury history and surgeries. You haven't played in three years. They are unsure if you can hold up." I replied quickly. "I don't understand, you just saw me workout. I'm in shape, I'm ready. You know me, you know my work ethic. Just give me an opportunity and I'll show you." I was passionate. He was blunt. "I wish we could. It sucks and not every coach agrees, but this is where we are now. Maybe if you play arena league or somewhere for a few games to get some current game film we can reevaluate you."

My heart raced for a different reason, my mind spinning, words tumbling out. "Are you kidding me?" We went back and forth. "We should sign you." What the heck does he mean? Of course they should. These are the same doctors who told me I would never play football again. Were they trying to prove a point? Arena ball? I'm a starting NFL running back." Words ran through my mind. Not one of these guys ever set foot on a field. Did he know who he was talking to? The reality of the NFL set in. Three years ago, I was a starting running back, who had beaten the odds, drafted out of a small school and played in the Super Bowl. I was on the verge of a life changing contract. But that was then, and this was now. What have you done for me lately? That was the motto. You're only as good as your last game or practice. Competition is intense, jobs on the line daily. Everyone looking for the next big thing, not for the guy who once had it. He could tell I was upset. I didn't hide it. I shook his hand without looking him in the eyes and stormed out the door. I wanted to scream. This was my time. I was ready. Ok, what's the next best move? God help me.

My mind regrouped. I suddenly felt calm. I thought: Go back in there, shake his hand again, look him in the eye and say thank you for the opportunity. Tell him, I'll be back. I felt ashamed, embarrassed, upset, but I knew this was the right thing to do. I walked back in the door and did the right thing. He looked surprised. He knew I was upset but he was confused about why I came back. I could see his wheels spinning. "You know what? I just heard of this league, the XFL. I don't know much about it, but I know a guy there. Let me give him a call and see what he knows."

My mind spun again. The XFL? Could this get any worse. First arena league and now some league no one has heard of. You can't be serious. I stood there fighting to maintain my composure. He made a call and I could hear his words. "Hey, I have a guy here, Tim Hightower. He played and started for us. He needs some game film. Do you guys have any openings? He just needs a few games to show he can still play. OK cool, I'll send him your number and tell him to call you, thanks." He turned to me. "They have a game Friday in New York. You could drive up there tomorrow, practice two days and play Friday." I had no clue what just happened, nor who he had called. I thanked him and walked out the door for good. Well, at least for the moment.

I had asked for an opportunity. This is not what I expected but here it was. I wasn't sure how to feel. I had completed an NFL workout. One step closer to returning to play. Yet, I was being told to play in the XFL. I did some research and could not find a legitimate website much less anyone who made it to the NFL from this experimental league. What do I have to lose? I called my agent. He would give sound advice. He got to the point. "Tim, I have never heard of this league. I can't recommend that you go. If you get hurt, you're not covered." Where did that opinion leave things? When you ask for advice, does that mean you follow it? Why did I ask in the first place? Was my mind already made up? Did I need him to validate something I knew?

I thought back to the time after the first surgery. Then I intended to return to the Washington training camp even though my body was not ready. I knew it, but I felt like the team was counting on me. Then Eugene begged, "Tim, do not step on that field until you are 100 percent healthy. They don't care about your progress, all that matters is that you step back on that field as good as you were before you went down." A part of me trusted him, but part of me was intent on proving everyone wrong. Sometimes your greatest strength becomes your greatest weakness. I did not need to prove Eugene wrong. I should have listened. I regret my decision.

Wise people put smarter people around them and listen to them. I had seen this from the veteran players I admired. The players who had long careers and success after their playing days had accountants, attorneys, mentors, trainers. They had a team of trusted advisors to help them make wise decisions and they listened. Most guys trusted friends. Some meant well yet were unqualified to give advice. Others believed the hype that because they made it to the NFL, they could figure it out. Success in football meant success in every area, they assumed.

Back in Washington's training camp after the initial surgery, I fell into this group. I was used to beating the odds. Why would this time be different? I can handle this. What I did not know was the business of football. I knew sports. I knew competition. I knew discipline, but I did not know business. Against Eugene's advice and my gut, I returned prematurely to the field. I struggled during training camp. Something was wrong. My body did not feel or operate the same. I went through the post practice interviews saying all the right things and projecting confidence in team trainers and medical professionals, but in my heart I felt different. I was concerned. As practices went on, my body felt worse. No matter how many early morning or late night treatments I took, nothing helped. I remember sitting in the head coach's office the day before I was cut. He mentioned how hard he saw me work to return to full health, how much of a leader I was, that he needed me and would give me time to get healthy.

Then I learned the business of football. The next morning, I was summoned upstairs to see the coach and released, cut from the team. What had changed? Actually nothing. Football is a business as well as a team sport. I replayed this tape in my mind, over and over, more vividly when I phoned Eugene to ask his advice about the XFL. Before I was cut, he had cautioned me not to try to play until I was fully healed.

As players we pride ourselves on toughness on the field. Knowing when to separate entertainment from business is a skill many learn too late. As a player I spent years learning when to evade a defender versus when to run through him; when to fight for an extra yard versus run out of bounds. I never grasped that an agent and other professionals spent their lives learning the art of deal making, finance and risk mitigation. No one can be an expert at everything. That's why true strength lies in knowing what you know and, more importantly, knowing what you don't know. Then you place people around you who do know and whom you can trust.

So again, I faced taking action against the advice of my agent. He was not adamant about going to the XFL, but he did not give his blessing. I paused to check my motivation. With Washington, in the past, I made a decision based on pride, fear of the unknown and trying to please others. The situation had changed. I was different. There was no ego in this decision, no pride and nothing to prove to anyone but myself. This was passion driven. I just wanted to be seen for who I was, for what I could do, then and there. That's all I asked for in the Washington tryout: see me for who I am. Yet it did not pan out. They could not look past the injury.

Was the XFL the way to go? Whatever it was, would this new league offer a way forward? I knew my motives were pure, yet I still was reluctant to make the decision. Then I remembered a dream told to me by my best friend a month earlier.

Brittney was my pastor's daughter and friend since the eighth grade. I don't remember when we became best friends. But, as years passed, we got to know each other's families and our personal dreams and ambitions. From day one the friendship clicked. It was effortless. I was very focused on football and school. I casually dated but was not interested in a lot of free time on the phone or weekends with someone. I was more interested in perfecting my craft. She never fought for attention yet when we saw each other, she listened, we laughed and enjoyed each other's company. We would talk about our life philosophies, debate perspectives and what we would be when we grew up. I did not have to say much, which I liked. She seemed to understand.

Brittney dreamed that someone phoned me to open a door back to the NFL. There was a way back after all. However, in order to walk through that door, I must do something unusual. Her dream did not specify. But it would be outlandish.

It was both a powerful and a puzzling dream. I listened at first because she is a friend. Then I was impatient. "None of this makes sense," I told her. "I'm not doing this with you." Brittney persisted even though I was at a low point. She had a message that went beyond this dream and that was even harder to hear.

"Tim nearly gave up on himself," Brittney said later. "He was struggling with whether or not to play, whether or not he would be able to play." She went to the hospital after the last surgery and spoke directly." "This is not it," she told me. "Football is meant to be a stepping- stone for something greater in your life."

Now I was really mad. What was she saying? What was she trying to do? I was focused on getting back to the NFL. Where was she coming from?

A few months later, when I was considering the odd idea of playing a game in the XFL, I remembered Brittney's dream. I had to tell her. "You will not believe. I got a call." Maybe it was the dream that pushed me forward. OK, I would try the XFL. But would this lead back to the NFL? Brittney had an immediate answer. "Next year you will be back and playing in the NFL." I certainly wanted to believe that. But how was that going to happen?

For the moment there was nothing more about football being a stepping-stone to something greater, as she put it. She was convinced. I was not and not ready to hear that. Washington had suggested the XFL, and I had scored a touchdown in that game. But they still refused to sign me. Where did that leave things? All the talk about getting game film seemed lost. "At least you played in a game," Brittney reasoned. That wasn't good enough. So where was the rest of her dream, and her prediction that in a year I would be playing in the NFL? How could that happen?

Out of the blue, a new door opened, just as Brittney's dream suggested it would.

Chapter Thirteen

CONSIDER THE COST

Brittney's dream had come true, up to a point. Washington had invited me to a tryout and I had done well. They hinted that some game film might eliminate doubt about my knee and my ability to compete. So, I played in an XFL game, even scoring a touchdown. It was cold and wet at the little field near Coney Island where I showed what I could do. Now what?

Was her dream incomplete? Did my dream fizzle? Washington still refused to sign me. I had nowhere else to turn. Then the phone rang. It was an unexpected call, from New Orleans. The Saints invited me to a tryout. I was back on the NFL radar.

It was another reminder: you never know when the opportunity will come or how it will appear. Your job is to stay committed to doing what you believe will lead you to your goal.

It was unlikely, especially later, when I heard the whole story. Nevertheless, it was an invitation. In a few days I flew to New Orleans. In and out for a day. Just enough time for a workout with other running backs the Saints were evaluating. Terry

Fontenot was Director of Pro Personnel for the Saints at that time. He recalls crucial details I would only learn later.

"We had a 'street list' of available players, beyond those who had been cut recently by other NFL teams," Fontenot explains. "Honestly, I don't know how Tim made our list. We knew about him, of course." I was lucky to get that plane ticket to New Orleans.

"The night before we brought those guys in, I reviewed the list. It dawned on me that Tim was coming. What were we doing? He had been out of football for several years. Oh well, I thought, let's see what he can do. We did not have any expectations." That was good. Terry did not realize how ready I was. He soon found out. "From the moment Tim arrived, we were excited. He is an amazing man. That workout, he tore it up. We were shocked."

It proved to be an important lesson: if you want something, you prepare for it. You live as if you already have it. But you cannot take it for granted. Our actions must align with our desires.

That is gratifying. Terry is a friend, and now he is General Manager of the Atlanta Falcons. He knows how to evaluate players quickly. His vivid memory helps to explain how things unfolded from that workout. The Saints invited me to the Organized Team Activities (OTAs), off-season workouts from April into June. These drills allow extended time to consider players who are under close scrutiny for a spot on the roster. Successful performance at the OTAs mean an invitation to training camp, the last step before making the team.

The night before offseason workouts began, I made a list. Why was I here? What would I accomplish? What was important? I refused to go back on the promise I made to myself and my wife. In the past, I had made promises, even said prayers in desperation, only to go back to business as usual when times were good. How quickly we forget the pain of poor choices and hard times. This time would be different. I would have to make different choices. I had to hold myself accountable. First up on the list, have a conversation with Coach Sean Payton. I needed to know why I was there. What was his vision? What was his expectation? For once I would develop a relationship with a coach instead of spending all my time trying to prove him wrong. As I arrived at the Saints practice facility, I smiled. This was really happening. I was part of a team again. I had a long way to go, but compared to how far I had come, this was a big deal.

Approaching Coach Payton's office, I paused to pray. "Thank you, God for bringing me to this point. I know you are with me." I approached his secretary who asked if he was expecting me. "No, just wanted a few minutes to speak with him," I said. As she walked away, I studied my list of questions, then nervously returned it to my pocket. When I went in, Coach Payton sat there with a big smile on his face.

"Coach, I just wanted to thank you for the opportunity, but I must be honest, I am a bit surprised and confused. Why did you bring me here? After all this time? There are many running backs out there. Why me? What is your plan?" Still smiling, he described seeing me play for Arizona and compared me to a few of his players from the past. He still recalls my eighty-yard touchdown run for Arizona against the Saints in a playoff game. So, I felt free to proceed. "Coach, I understand that I am at a different point in my career. I'm older and I understand the business of football. All I ask is that you are straight with me. I do not want to hear anything from the media, I want to hear it from you. I promise I will give you the same respect. You have my total effort and commitment each day, no off-field distractions, and no surprises. You will be the first to know." His smile broadened and he shook my hand.

I was working my way down the list of things to do. Now, earn the respect of my teammates and coaching staff, be in the best shape of my life, and find the hardest worker on the team. The last part proved easy. Day after day, I watched Drew Brees arrive early in the morning and only leave in the evening. He approached his daily warmup with a playoff focus. Where most guys took it easy in the offseason, this veteran quarterback refused to miss a practice. It was the attention to detail that left a strong impression. Every play, after the ball was thrown, he would scan the field to make sure everyone was in the right spot. What he ate, how he watched film, his training regimen. Everything had purpose and discipline. I had considered myself a hard worker. I would often refer to my college days going from offseason football workouts straight to basketball practice followed by track practice. With Drew, it was more than seeing how hard he could push his body. He challenged himself mentally, in the film room, the training room and in the cafeteria. He focused on winning.

Soon even Brad, the chef in the team cafeteria, knew me. I had unusual requests for him. The first day, at breakfast, was our introduction. "May I have five egg whites, onions, jalapenos, extra kale, tomatoes, sea salt and salmon? Oh, and can you cook it in this avocado oil please?" I took out a packet of salmon and a bottle of avocado oil and handed them to Brad. He smiled and agreed. The look on his face told me that he was not used to such personalized instructions." Food had become medicine to me. A few months earlier I had been rushed to the hospital. Days later, Dr. Mellman prescribed a strict diet. The foods were meant to heal my body from the inside. Everything was detailed and specific. I was to cook only with avocado, almond and sesame oil. No pepper. Lots of Bison and wild caught salmon. It seemed crazy but it worked. I became as lean as I had ever been with no pain or inflammation in my knee. Less than a year removed from the last surgery, I could not take any chances.

Not everything was going so smoothly. There was a nagging issue that had become huge. The Saints provided meals and a small stipend at the OTA, but no place to stay. Players were on their own. That presented a problem and it became central each time Rikki and I spoke.

"I'm ok" I told her. "How are the kids. Do you guys have what you need?" She had questions of her own. "Tim, is there anywhere else you can go? There has to be somewhere." I was steadfast. "I will be ok, Rikki. This is all part of a bigger purpose." At times I could shift her focus with a motivating speech reminding her of the big picture or reminding her of a time back in high school or college where I faced insurmountable odds but somehow managed to overcome. This is why she married me right? Because she could rely on me to come through in the tough times. I had to remain strong mentally and emotionally. I would not let her know that deep down I was worried and I was tired. I was not at the point of giving up, but emotionally I was drained. Why did I need to pretend? Maybe she knew. Maybe I should tell her how I felt. But that's not what I saw, that's not what I knew. My father had been in worse times and I never saw him cry. He prayed and believed the best would happen. But did I want to be like my father?

My questions poured out to Rikki. "Did you guys eat? Do you have food for breakfast?" All that mattered to me was that my family was ok. Just the thought of them going without food or shelter brought back painful childhood memories. I remember what it felt like as a kid, not knowing where our next meal would come from or where we would lay our head the next night. Even when my parents tried to remain calm, my siblings and I felt the tension. We knew things were not right, yet there was nothing we could do. As I grew older, I told myself that I would never allow my family to go without. That will never happen. Yet, look at where I had to sleep.

As I lay in the car, I could feel it shaking, rocking back and forth. Rain hit the windows from all sides. I tried to cover the phone as I talked so she could not hear the severity of the storm. I did not want her to worry. She had been strong for the last four years. It seemed like yesterday we were strolling happily down the aisle. We recited our handwritten vows pledging to be there for each other through thick and thin. But did we really know what that meant? In the next four years, I would lose my job, have multiple surgeries, spend all the money, and see my wife lose her mother. We would have kids while trying to figure out who we were and what love really meant. Would we still say, "I do?" Rikki went from being carried in a Bentley coupe on her way to paradise to carrying me down the hall to the emergency room, carrying her mother to hospice and carrying our first son. I couldn't ask her to carry any more.

Yet the truth had to be faced. "Tim, I don't feel comfortable with you sleeping in your car." I was resolute. "What other choice do I have Rikki?" I promised her that if the storm got worse, I would move somewhere safer though I had no clue where that would be. "Give the kids a kiss for me. I will talk to you in the morning, I love you." But there would be no sleep this night. I prayed as I often saw my father do. "God, protect me. Protect my family. I know you did not bring me here to leave me now. I don't understand but I trust you. Get me through these times and help me to use this story to inspire others. Amen." I tried to wrap my mind around what was happening. Is this the price one must pay to pursue a dream? The storm intensified. It was June, which meant the beginning of hurricane season in New Orleans. A season filled with high winds, heavy rain, tornadoes, flooding and power outages. We were in the middle of offseason workouts. The storm had begun earlier in the day, knocking out all power at the Saints facility. Players were sent home. But, I did not have a home.

Off and on, I had a room in an extended stay hotel. My family was back in Richmond and most of what I made was sent back to take care of rent, utilities and groceries. I could eat for free during the day at the practice facility and would make a to-go box to eat for dinner. During the day I was living a dream. I had overcome all odds and returned to the NFL after almost four years away. But at night I was reminded of what it cost to get me there. I knew this before I left Richmond to begin this journey. I wrote down what it took for my family to live. Rent, food, insurance, daycare, utilities, transportation, and debt. Everything came out to about six grand monthly. While at the OTAs, I would receive $6,400 a month. If there were no unexpected expenses, I could almost cover home base. I would make it work.

I figured out how to stagger payments. I hated the idea of being irresponsible, but told myself I could buy time until September, when the real checks came in. But if I did not make the team, what would I do? I did not have time for what ifs. I had no other choice. I must make this team. I learned that if I at least paid my rent and a portion of my utilities that would buy me time until the next check came. All other bills would have to be paid every other month. We were in survival mode. You never understand the choices people make until you are in a situation where you must survive. Your motivation is not to cheat anyone or be dishonest but to take care of your family. It's as instinctive as breathing.

A few days out of the week I would check in to an extended stay. I was always behind in payments. I would return to my room, find out my key was not working, and go to the front desk only to find out "Mr. Hightower, the card we have on file did not work." I would make up some excuse as to why and promise them I would contact my bank. "Probably has something to do with me being out of town so much," I would say. They never called me out so I stayed with my story. They knew I was an NFL player so there was no way I could not afford a $75 a night tab. The front desk lady would often joke with me. Sometimes the stereotypes weren't a bad thing.

There were no jokes this time. I had already checked out of the room and had no place to go. All day I had an empty place in my stomach knowing that night would come and I would have to decide. Where would I park my car to sleep? I decided to park not far from the practice facility. I would not risk being late the next morning and just in case things got really bad I could always return there. I could arrive early the next morning before anyone arrived, shower and be ready to go. Maybe it would work to my favor. Hey, I was the first one there and the last one to leave. Hardest worker on the team. Checked that box. Seemed like a solid plan.

I turned the car off to preserve gas, turned off phone notifications and reclined my seat. The car rocked back and forth. I sat up and looked around. I could see nothing. Rain covered the windows on all sides. The wind started blowing so heavily

I feared something would fly through the window, so I started the engine and moved to the center of the parking lot. Away from trees and objects that could be thrown by the storm. Tears flooded my eyes. I remembered being a kid and sleeping in hotels and friends' basements. How did things come full circle and I end up here? What did I do wrong? I don't deserve to be here. I worked my butt off in high school. I avoided parties and instead hit the track. Not once but twice I beat the odds. Why am I here?

When I went down in October 2011, I made a decision: whatever it took, I would get back. As I recalled this commitment, I asked myself: "Is this what it takes to accomplish something great"? Angry, nervous, scared, I realized that I still wanted it. I thought about the surgeries, the countless doctors' visits. Then I thought about the call from my agent, Eugene Parker. "Tim, the Saints want to sign you." One yes was worth one thousand nos. One answered prayer brought more happiness than four years of pain. In the midst of a storm, I could smile. I realized that what was in me was stronger than anything that could ever happen to me. I was more than the loss of finances or the loss of a job. I was more than my worst nightmare. I had overcome my greatest fears. Two things remained, the love of my wife and my love for the game of football. I said one more prayer, "Thank you God" and closed my eyes.

When off-season workouts were over, I went home to my family to take a break. Then, it was back to New Orleans for training camp. There was only one problem: I was out of money. Every dollar had been sent to Richmond to keep things going while I was away. I had overstayed my welcome at the extended stay. So, I reached out to a fellow teammate, C. J. Spiller. C. J. was a fellow running back who had purchased a home in New

Orleans. He allowed me stay at his place for a bit. I made up an excuse about me needing to stay longer to train.

Meanwhile I had to figure out how to get $600 for a flight. After phoning a few people, I reached out to my brother and sister. I was overcome by pride and embarrassment. Here I was the professional athlete, borrowing money from my older brother and sisters. Early in my career, they came to me for assistance. Now the tables were turned. I had not shared with them every detail of my journey over the last few years, but they understood. Without hesitation they both agreed to wire me money. "You did the same for us," they said. That is what families do. Despite the earlier differences, family was there for me. Things were beginning to align.

There was another sign of change. In my freshman year of college, I told my teammates that I wanted to win and would do whatever it took. We would win a National Championship, I told them. We had come off a 3–8 season. Some laughed, others rolled their eyes, but everyone heard. I declared that I would not cut my hair until we won a National Championship. I needed their attention, I wanted them to feel my intensity.

I had no clue how much my hair would take on an identity of its own. It became a part of me and what I represented. For my mother, the decision to grow my hair was one more reason to be profiled negatively: Black, athlete, long hair. I stood out enough, I did not need any more negative attention. She pleaded with me not to grow it. I could not understand her concern. I was a college kid. I kept my nose clean as much as possible. Why should I change my appearance to appease someone who probably didn't want me there anyway? I never imagined being profiled six years later and nearly arrested, because my hair fit the description of a wanted criminal.

The longer my hair grew the more questions I was asked. It connected me to others with dreadlocks. I began to learn the history of dreadlocks, the culture, the strength. It became an identity. I no longer cared about the way I was perceived. My hair was a part of who I was. It brought me pride. In part, it was a rebellion. Who created the standard of acceptable hair styles and what was wrong with mine? As we advanced through the playoffs my senior year at Richmond, I felt nervous. But I was not ready to cut my hair. In my first few years in the NFL, my hair became an identity. It became my brand. In the football world my accomplishments on the field and my image off the field challenged stereotypes often associated with Black athletes with dreadlocks. Once I no longer was a professional athlete, people were less willing to give me the benefit of the doubt. A principal avenue to acceptance had been removed.

As I returned home from New Orleans, I thought about a recent vow I made. I told my wife things would be different, that I was different. I believe true change starts within, with a definitive decision. I also believe in symbolism. I had not cut my hair since the vow I made ten years prior. The time had come to create a new image. I was not the same kid who went down on that football field. Something had changed inside of me, and I wanted the change reflected on the outside. I was not reluctant to cut my hair. The anticipation of what lay ahead was greater than the fear of what was left behind. As each lock fell, I recalled a familiar Bible passage: "Old things have passed away, behold all things have become new" (2 Corinthians 5:17).

The door was opening in New Orleans. The time spent, and even the need to sleep in the car moved life ahead. But life rarely is straight forward. There were more complications. I would need patience and inner strength. Training camp had gone well. So well that Sean Payton said the magic words late in the summer of 2015: "Tim, you made the team." Then things went downhill. The day after, team doctors gave me an injection designed to "boost" the knee for the season. But it backfired. By the eve of the first game of the season, the knee was completely swollen.

This was more irony and agony than I could absorb. The first Saints' game would be against the Cardinals in Arizona, my first team. I had practically begged Payton to let me play. I told him I would do anything, including special teams. Then it was in doubt. A small number of people have reactions to this injection, I was told. Did this mean the knee was infected again?

Dr. Josh Sandell back in Minnesota was reassuring. It was not infected but it had become inflamed. Realigning the hips and ankles would stimulate healing. A few weeks would be needed but the body would bounce back. I trusted these words. After years of treatments of all sorts I had found what worked for me. It wasn't the same body as it had been seven years before, as a rookie at Arizona. I moved differently. More time was needed to warm up before practice and to stretch between practices. It was frustrating. But I had made the team. Then the knee flared.

I had been overjoyed at making the team. I called Rikki immediately. "We did it," I shouted. We needed to celebrate this moment together. Rikki had driven me to over fifty doctors' visits, pushed me in a wheelchair after surgeries, and packed our belongings to move from house to house without a single complaint. We needed to celebrate.

Next, I called my mother. With her I let out more of my feelings. I told her what I could not yet tell Rikki: that I was angry and confused. My body was not the same even when the knee was not swollen. Summer workouts revealed that I needed more repetition. Over nearly four years, the carefully cultivated instincts of an NFL player had not been maintained. They needed to be rebuilt and the body was older. Still, I had gotten there, hadn't I? They could be rebuilt, couldn't they? As I asked these questions, I found that the knee was swollen yet again.

"Tim, we are going to sign you then release you prior to the game." Coach Payton's words hit like a hammer blow. Just when it seemed that life was coming together, it fell apart. I did not know what to feel. The relief that I made the team was overshadowed by this message. More than injury and recovery, physical condition or performance were involved. I was nearing the wrong side of thirty-years old. The situation became a business calculation. What mattered were the odds of how many years I might have left and the economics that a team could get two younger, less expensive players for the price of one veteran. Cold, hard fact.

I had lost a lot of time, four years to be exact. The comeback did not mean hitting the reset button. I could not be twenty-one again. My body was different, so my role with a team would be different. I wanted to pick up where I left off in Carolina. But I could no longer be a starting running back on the verge of a life-changing contract. I could either fight reality or create a new vision.

There was no fighting the reality of being released. I had been on the verge of being a New Orleans Saint when the knee acted up. I knew things would work out, but when? It was more apparent how it might work out. The same way a running back got a chance when I was injured. Hopeful free agents do not watch NFL games to root for a favorite team. Phone in hand, they watch to see if an injury will open up a roster spot. It is the reality of football as a business.

My friend Brittney remained confident. The dream did not die. She was prepared to act. She purchased tickets to the Saints-Tennessee Titans game in early November, near her birthday. I could not stop her. All I could do was stay in playing shape in Richmond. The rest was beyond my control.

On November 1, 2015, the New Orleans Saints played the New York Giants. I watched the first quarter then had to stop. Rikki is a better sports fan. I left to run errands. While I was at a grocery store, she texted: Saints' running back Khiry Robinson broke his leg in the game.

Within one hour, Terry Fontenot phoned. The Saints needed me in New Orleans right away. It seemed that Brittney might watch me play for her birthday after all.

Chapter Fourteen

PREPARE AS IF

The realization of Brittney's dream was not the end of the story. It began a new phase of my journey. As I struggled to heal and to return to the NFL, I found a new mindset: prepare "as if." I had to be ready at every moment for the opportunity to play. It would dawn on me later that there would other opportunities, off the field, for which I must prepare. In time, Brittney's vision of living beyond football would also come true.

I was learning to see my situation in a certain way: preparing "as if." Things were unstable but hopeful. I didn't have a guaranteed contract, but I was motivated. I needed stability. There had been so much instability. Rikki and I had moved from home to home since 2012 and gotten married as I chased the dream of returning to football. Although I had been released before the first game of the season, I believed that I would be brought back. Then every week would be essentially a tryout. How well I performed each week was the issue. I had to be ready.

It was tough. But the tension put me back in that mindset of not being able to take even one practice for granted. My football life was one day at a time. I felt like a rookie again. I felt like a kid in high school and college. I tapped memories of earlier successes and rediscovered lessons learned. Key life principles can be easily forgotten. I had to regain the old sense of challenge. If not, I may not have gotten another chance. This was the only window I would have.

As I worked to maximize the opportunity, I was fortunate. My family was all in. Also, there were fewer distractions. I didn't have the same challenges that I faced in my first few NFL years. It was no longer hard to tell people "No." I was finished with that stress. Now, I knew that I had a precious opportunity. Not that I didn't understand it before, but my sense of priority had become clear. I could no longer fly family and close friends to games. I could not give many gifts. Now, my sleep, my training, everything had to be on point. It was much harder as a young player to say "No," or to divide my focus by giving various people my time. Now, I was focused on maximizing my opportunity with the Saints.

After I was released, I spent time with Dr. Josh Sandell in Minnesota. He knew exactly what to do with my body. In a matter of weeks, I was feeling like myself, ready to go again. It became a matter of waiting for opportunity to come. Then the Saints' called after Khiry was injured. I came back, worked out, and felt great. But where would I fit in? How would I make my mark? In my first game, feelings were mixed. It was a battle between being grateful to be back and not being satisfied. How do you straddle being appreciative while pushing to overcome the remaining hurdles? You have to challenge yourself, not being complacent, because you know how hard it is to get where you want to go.

But, when you've been out, you realize how many people are gunning for your job, how many people would love to trade places with you. You can't rely on what you did yesterday. Yet you must be thankful for the moment. That's what I felt each day at practice, taking advantage of the moment while preparing as if my day would come, that I would get a chance to start again.

At practice, I often stood behind the starting running back while he got all the first-team reps. The other running backs would get the second-team reps. But I would stand behind the starter in the huddle. I would close my eyes and picture myself in that huddle. When they clapped their hands to break the huddle, I would clap my hands. I would imagine that I was getting that first-team role every single day after practice. I would get the practice script and I would run through every play on my own as if that was my play. I prepared "as if."

In the first game, the reality of being back sank in, just as my friend, Brittney, had dreamed. She and her husband came to the game. We faced the Tennessee Titans and I only played on special teams. I may have played one or two plays in offense. Even with playing in an NFL game again, I was not satisfied. I wasn't content. Yet, I kept thinking, what's wrong with me? Why am I not grateful? When we lost, I was upset. I hate losing and I wanted to play. I wanted to contribute in a major way. Fortunately, part of coming back is having those strong people around me, especially Rikki and Brittney and her husband.

Brittney's dream came at a crucial time. Less than a year before reaching the Saints, I was lying in a hospital bed, wondering if I would get another opportunity. Then I played in a football game, my first in four years. I needed perspective. As

I continued to challenge myself to improve those persons who knew me best provided perspective. I especially needed their support in my second game back. For that game, the Saints went to Washington, my hometown.

This is where it had started, and this is where I had left off. I wanted to leave a mark, but that game did not go well. We were blown out by Washington. At first, I didn't play much, mostly special teams. But in the fourth quarter, Coach Payton put me in the game at running back. I was a man on a mission. I had something to prove. It was the first time I played in a football game without getting tired. Three, four, even five carries of the ball in a row. I had focus and drive. It was a now-or-never, one-shot mentality. One opportunity mentality is something I will never lose. You can never be complacent, no matter how far you go.

After the Washington game, I learned that our starting running back, Mark Ingram, hurt his shoulder and was out for the season. Khiry Robinson already was gone for the season. C. J. Spiller, our other running back, had come back from injury but was not at full speed. As the injury list grew, we were headed into a game with a key rival, the Tampa Bay Buccaneers. It was important even though the season seemed pretty much lost.

There was no one else for the Saints to count on but me. I was told a few days before the game that I would start. I wasn't nervous. It was an opportunity that I almost expected. Still, it was a tough place to be. I respected Mark. I respected Khiry. It was hard to realize that the only reason I had fresh opportunity was because someone else had been hurt. At first, I felt guilty. It was easy to think that I got this job because someone else went down. But I resolved not to feel bad. Who cares how I got there? What I would do with the opportunity is what mattered.

I resolved to make the most of this opportunity. I was prepared to take full advantage of this moment. My body was in shape. I had trained. I knew the playbook. When I warmed up my hamstring was a little tight, but that worked itself out. There was no hint that I would have a record-breaking day and that I would carry the ball more in this game than in any previous game in my career. In the fourth quarter, I lived a dream. I could not imagine it being better.

It was a tight game against Tampa Bay, a rival in our division of the NFL, before their home crowd. We took the lead, and then, late in the game, we went into what's called four-minute mode. When your team has a lead late in the game, the strategy is to run the ball, keep the clock running and protect the football. Do not lose control of the ball. Do not stop the clock. Keep the ball going, keep making first downs, force the other team to utilize their timeouts. To make this happen, the running back must be trusted. Play after play, he must carry the ball. He must know when to fight for extra yards, and when to get down, staying in bounds, so the clock does not stop. A high level of trust in the running back is key. He must carry the ball again and again. That's what Coach Payton did. He put the ball in my hands play after play.

My passion grew, as did my focus and determination. I refuse to lose this opportunity. Even when my body started to get tired, I could hear Kyle Shanahan's words four years earlier: "Tim, I'm putting this game on your shoulder." So, I did not relent. I told my body, one more carry, one more, one more. Tim, this is your time. You've earned this. They're counting on you. You can do this. I talked to myself over and over. All of a sudden, it was third down. This meant that either we got a first down, to keep the ball and win the game, or we were forced to punt the ball back to Tampa Bay. Then they would have a chance to win the game.

I remember, when I was carrying the ball, someone pulling my jersey. At that moment, an extra strength went through me, and I pulled through. An opponent ripped my jersey but I got the first down and we nailed down the win. I got down on one knee when the game ended. My first start in coming back ended with a win on the road. I was emotionally overwhelmed. I ran to that locker room and got there ahead of anyone else. I was overtaken with emotions. I wanted to embrace every team member. Until then, I had not been a very vocal player. I kept to myself. When a person is quiet, you may not realize what that person has gone through. You may never know a person's story or their struggle.

At this point, I let it all out. I shook every hand. I hugged every coach, every player. I'll never forget that feeling. When Coach Payton reached our huddle in the locker room, I took over and I screamed. In part, Payton is a good coach because he knows when to let his players lead. He knew what that game meant to me personally. He allowed me to lead that team down the field in the fourth quarter, and then again in the locker room after the game.

What meant even more than scoring that touchdown and sealing the game in the fourth quarter was the respect I received from coaches, from fans, from teammates. The comments stick with me to this day. It was everything that I craved because in professional football you play to earn the respect of those around you. It can only be earned by hard work. It meant a great deal when I felt a new depth of respect, including from my family. I wanted my recovery to represent something important for other people. I felt that as we closed out the season. We finished the year by winning three out of four games, and I rushed for nearly a hundred yards in each game.

It was a feeling I could not lose after that Tampa Bay game. I wanted to stay in this moment. You never know how long you can hold the feeling. You try to hold onto it for as long as possible. As a team, that's what we did for the remainder of that season. However, there was uncertainty. I was still on a one-year contract. The year had been a Cinderella story for me. I won the FedEx ground player of the week for the best running back performance. Then, in my second start, against the Jacksonville Jaguars, I rushed for two touchdowns and 122 yards carrying the ball. It seemed like a true comeback.

But uncertainty lingered. What would happen after the season? Would I be one and done again? I didn't know how long this opportunity would extend. So, in the off-season, the issue with my agent was what teams valued me. It was a reminder that as great as I felt coming off that year, I was still a running back on the wrong side of thirty years old and I had faced multiple knee surgeries. I wasn't in my prime. Although I did everything I could on the field, I was still a statistic. That deeply frustrated me.

As much as I tried to focus on what was ahead, it was hard not to think about the strikes against me. There were constant reminders of the reality of the time that was lost and how that affected my chances. The most gratifying part about that whole season was winning the NFL's Ed Block courage award in the off-season. I had also hoped for the Walter Payton comeback player of the year award but didn't win it for the NFL. Still, the Saints gave me the team comeback award and then I won the Ed Block award. Seeing the stories of so many guys who had overcome adversity and being connected to the sponsoring foundation at the ceremony in Baltimore meant a great deal to me. Kids and people in the community who have overcome insurmountable odds were honored. I shared the platform with them and could do so with my family there. My own children could see me receive an award that represented more than just me. It represented perseverance and resilience. It represented overcoming something that was not supposed to be overcome. Even more, it was a sign about my future that I continued to explore.

The award meant that anything is possible. I wanted to be back in New Orleans. Where else would I be? This team wanted me. No one else did. But I was reminded that football is a business. New Orleans liked me. Coach Payton liked me. Mickey Loomis, the general manager, liked me. But they offered me another one-year deal, a minimum deal for a veteran player. I was frustrated. I had earned the right to play, to be a starter. I had shown that I could contribute at a high level when called upon. But I was still learning that football is both a game and a business.

In this business, and in any business, the emphasis is on leverage. I didn't have any leverage. No team was willing to sign me to a long-term contract. No other team was willing to pay above the minimum. They didn't have to. I was a running back nearing thirty, with five knee surgeries. I was a liability. I fought and I pleaded. I was looking for that long-term contract, similar to what I had before I was injured. No team was willing to assume that risk. They didn't see me as I wanted to be seen. So, while they liked me as a player, they weren't willing to overcompensate from a business perspective.

Once more with New Orleans, I went into training camp for the 2016 season uncertain about my place on the roster. I was not assured of making the team. Even when I made the roster, Coach Payton gave me the same message as he had a year earlier: we're going to have to release you for the first game. Well, I wasn't okay with that. At this point, I had a good relationship with Payton, so I took a risk and told him directly: I don't feel comfortable with that. I was direct: if you release me, I'm going to look to sign with another team. So, he chose not to release me. But, I did not play well. I'm not sure why. My hunger was there but I didn't play well. I had become more nervous about the opportunity to play than hungry for it. The hunger had become elusive; I did not know how to get it back. Hunger can easily turn into fear. It can be traced back to the passion involved in pursuing success. It can lead to irrational vulnerability and then to fear. I had been vulnerable to so many people for so long.

Without realizing it, you can become fearful of making a mistake, and the fear cripples. It halts your trust in your ability to perform. That's what I felt that season. I had a few high points, but mostly I became afraid of making mistakes. I had never felt that before when I played the game. When the 2016 season was over, there were more questions than ever. We did not make the playoffs. We won seven games and lost nine. Again, I wondered what the future would be.

As I considered what my future would be, something troubling happened. I was in the midst of wondering about the Saints and what my legacy would be when there was a profound loss. It concerned my agent, Eugene Parker. Up to this point, Eugene and I had been close. He treated his clients as good friends. He communicated clearly and often. He always had a plan for me, and I knew where I stood. Then, I heard that Eugene was sick. I did not understand how sick. He only let people who were very close, such as his family and a few long-time players know how sick he was. I hadn't been in touch with him for a while. So, I didn't know where I stood with other teams. I didn't have any visits lined up. This was unusual for Eugene.

While I was training in Arizona, I felt led. My gut said to call the Saints' general manager and to meet with him personally. I felt that I needed to take matters into my own hands. At this point, I was learning to trust my gut, trust my instinct. I sent the GM a message and set a time to meet. Before I went to New Orleans, I met with Jack Ross to go over my approach. Jack was a former attorney. I wanted his help in preparing to negotiate on my own behalf. Jack and I researched all the running backs out there, the free agents, what the compensation would be, what the salary caps would be. The work prepared me to negotiate. But, as I was about to fly to New Orleans to negotiate with the Saints, I received a text from my former general manager at Arizona, Rod Graves: "Tim, I'm sorry to hear about Eugene Parker."

What was this? I didn't know that Eugene Parker had died. I looked it up and sure enough. Then I made some calls. He died on the day before I was to meet with the Saints. Such a loss. I was heartbroken. It had been good to trust my gut and prepare on my own. But I was devastated for Eugene and for his family. Selfishly, I also was troubled about what this meant for me. He was the guy who I trusted. He was the guy that I knew and who knew me.

I went to New Orleans to meet with Mickey Loomis, the general manager. Before entering the Saints' facility, I said a quick prayer, just as I did a year earlier before seeing Coach Payton. Then I looked at my notes and took a deep breath. I was nervous. This was the first time I was negotiating on my own behalf. When I walked into that office though, I could see that Mickey Loomis, the general manager, was nervous. He explained to me about needing to make a business decision. He added that it was nothing personal. I was not upset. In fact, the more we spoke, the more comfortable I became. While it's a business, people run a business and Mickey is a good person. Nevertheless, halfway through that conversation, it was clear that I was getting nowhere. He was sticking with his position, and I was committed to my position.

Then, though I am not sure why, I asked him what success would look like for him? I added that my goal was to make the team with more than a minimum salary. If I give you what you want, will you give what I want? Mickey agreed. That became a first lesson in business negotiating. It isn't about getting my way all the time and proving to someone that things would be done in my way. It requires understanding what the other person wants and discovering how I can get what I want by giving them what they want. While it came on unexpected terms, it was a key lesson in business and in life. I negotiated incentives, bonuses, which I had not received previously. There had been no incentive bonuses in my contract. But there was more negotiation, this time with Payton. With him, part of the lesson that emerged was knowing when to fight and knowing when to listen and knowing who is for you, separating from those who are not for you. Let those who are for you, like Payton, make suggestions. Then listen to what is actually said.

Payton surprised me. He asked, "What do you think about playing fullback? Would you ever consider playing fullback?" His question revived an old memory. In high school, the coach had told me that I would never be a running back, that in college they would want to move me to fullback. It was a change in position that I was unwilling to accept then or later, with the

Saints. I resisted instead of considering who was giving this message. This was Sean Payton. He was the only person who took a chance on me. He had been truthful. We had developed a rapport. Yet, his question triggered my defense mechanism: I'm going to prove you wrong. This old message got in the way. I didn't consider that my deeper goal was to play three to four more years in the NFL. Payton saw an opportunity for me to evolve, to get what I wanted by another route. He understood that life is learning to adapt. He wanted me to evolve in order to prolong my career.

Unfortunately, I was unwilling to do that. Instead, I approached San Francisco. I heard that Kyle Shanahan had received the head coaching job for the 49ers. I remembered the last conversation I had with him. He was the last coach to see me as a starting running back. Maybe I could pick up where I left off. At times we all want to go back to an old relationship, to see if there is still a spark, still a connection. If we are honest, rarely do any flickers remain. When something has gone, it is over, rarely does anything worthwhile come out of trying to rekindle. What was life then is not now. It is not possible or desirable to go there. The future cannot be a revival of the past. Yet, I made a decision looking back instead of considering what would be the best decision going forward. I had been a 49ers fan as a kid. So, I reached out to Coach Shanahan. I consider him a friend. I hoped the door might in San Francisco.

When we spoke, I explained the situation to Coach Shanahan. I wasn't sure if Coach Payton thought I had a future in New Orleans, not the future I wanted. I felt Shanahan would give me a chance to play in a place that helped to nurture my childhood dream. I knew it was meant to be. It was destined to happen. So, I went to training camp in San Francisco. But, from the beginning, it didn't feel right. There was not the fit there had been in New Orleans. The Saints had seen opportunity. Shanahan had a different vision. No matter how hard I worked, the 49ers were rebuilding with younger players. That did not include me.

I remember being released from the team at the end of training camp. I had been so ready for this to work that I had moved my family out to the Bay Area. Then, there I was, sitting in Shanahan's office. He told me I was released, and I wanted to cry. It reminded me of five years earlier when I met with his dad, Mike Shanahan, then the coach in Washington. He told me that I was a part of the team. The next day he released me. It was the same feeling. I felt betrayed.

But I was more upset with myself because I made a decision based on pride. I had tried to prove a point instead of making the best decision for my family. Tears flood my eyes at this realization. Hard questions pressed me: What would be next? Where would I go? What would I do? I had just bought a house in Richmond, Virginia. I was banking on the fact that I would spend the next year on my childhood favorite team. But here I was again, out of work with no opportunities. I needed to find new direction.

Chapter Fifteen

SEEKING AND FINDING

What did I miss? What did I do wrong? How did I end up here again, so quickly? This is not how I expected the comeback story to end. Tears flooded my eyes as I held the personalized jersey in hand. I was so close to fulfilling a dream. As a child, I had imagined playing for the 49ers one day. Now, the dream vanishing, I tried to gather myself. Rikki walked in the door as I was bent over on the floor. She looked at me intently. Then she saw the personalized, 49ers' jersey she had ordered as a gift. It was intended to celebrate my making the San Francisco roster. A wonderful gift, motivated by love. But my brief time with the 49ers had ended.

I stood up and pulled myself together, reassuring her I was fine even though I wasn't. I was in pain and shock, confused and angry. I could hear my sons, Sir Lennox and Prince Ezra, knocking on the door, "Daddy, what's wrong." Quickly I wiped my tears and opened the door. I wanted to be in the moment but did not feel comfortable crying, grieving in front of my sons.

179

I was their superhero; they needed me to be strong, I thought. Images of what I saw growing up took over even when I wanted to be someone different. I needed time to process what had happened. I needed to live in the present. So, I went for a drive to clear my head, as I often did.

As I drove, a thought came to mind. Maybe this was yet another test. How badly did I want it? How much was I willing to struggle to become a 49er? Then I asked myself: what would I have done if I had made the team? The answer was obvious: I would celebrate with my family. I quickly made a U-turn and went to the closest Whole Foods store. There I picked up a gluten-free carrot cake and two red candles representing the number 22, the number I would have worn. I had come too far to give up now. The 49ers had made a terrible mistake. Surely they would call to offer me a spot on the roster and I would be ready when they did. Prepare as if, I thought. That worked before, why not now? I replayed the scenario in my mind, even looking at my phone anticipating the call from the team. I closed my eyes and imagined the feeling. As my head spun, I headed home to celebrate. I would show them what resilience looks like. As I pulled in the parking garage, I said a prayer, "I trust you did not bring me this far to leave me. I believe." I looked in the rearview mirror, practiced my smile then headed inside.

As I walked in the door, cake in hand, smile on my face, Rikki smiled. Had I received good news while I was out? "I knew they would call you back," she said warmly. "They did not," I told her. "But I believe they will. Let's celebrate in anticipation." Despite the look of confusion, Rikki gathered the kids to meet me in the kitchen. "Daddy, what are we celebrating?" Sir Lennox asked. "We are celebrating Daddy making the team," I said, trying to sound confident. Sir Lennox pressed his question. "Did you make the team?" "Not yet," I said. "But I believe I will." More questions followed. "But why are we celebrating if it did not happen?" Sir Lennox asked. I had a ready response. "Because when you believe in something, you prepare for it. You anticipate it even when no one else can see it or believe it. Daddy believes it and so we are preparing for it." He could not comprehend. I could only hope he would remember this lesson later when he would need it.

Even with the best intentions and one of the best gluten-free carrot cakes I had ever eaten, I could not shake the heavy feeling. Did I not believe in myself? I had already beaten the odds. Couldn't I do it once more? I tried everything to gain the "right" perspective. Hadn't I learned during those four years away from football it wasn't always about trying to find the right perspective or ignoring the reality of the pain I was experiencing. Sometimes I just needed to be present. To experience the emotions. To feel hurt, be angry, to cry, to acknowledge uncertainty. To ask for help. It was from the depths of these emotions that true resolve is born. It must be a process. Recovery becomes a journey. Resilience means hanging in there.

Over the next few days, my mood became worse. I refused to answer the phone. I had run out of motivational Instagram posts. In fact, I was starting to run out of motivation altogether. Then I thought back to October of 2011. How I refused to be helped off the field, refused to be seen by a team trainer, refused to acknowledge my knee was hurt, then refused to get the surgery. I thought about the challenges in my relationship with Rikki that often stemmed from my refusal to articulate the pain I was experiencing. My refusal to ask friends and family for help. Then it hit me: my strength had not come from being fearless. It had not come from being perfect. It came from acknowledging the pain of what happened, from being present in the moment. I could only locate where I wanted to go after I acknowledged where I was.

True recovery started the day I was no longer afraid to face reality. I was reminded of the lesson learned while sleeping in the car during off-season workouts. Then I began to cry. No more guarding every emotion, no more rigid idea of who I should be and what I should feel. I could not stop crying. My body started to shake. This cry was different. It hurt. Like something was being pulled from my body. It was a time of catharsis like I had never felt before. Finally, I was motionless as feelings washed over me.

After what seemed like hours I looked over at the personalized jersey. But this time a different thought came to mind. I would not throw it away nor would I be embarrassed by it. Maybe the jersey did not have to represent disappointment. Maybe it could serve as a reminder of what it took to go where I had gone, to achieve what I had achieved. The lessons learned, the sacrifice. The price you must pay to pursue your dreams. Maybe these realizations could serve as a new definition of recovery. Recovery, ultimately, does not mean trying to return to a past moment in time but creating new moments. The image that drove me as a kid, seeing my name on the back of a professional jersey, would now serve a different purpose. In a new way, a way I had never imagined before, I would move forward.

"Are you OK?" Rikki asked as she walked into the room. My answer came quickly. "No, not right now, but I believe I will be. Thank you for buying this jersey. It may have served a different purpose than you had intended, but maybe it was exactly what I needed." Just as I did three years prior when I first received the call from New Orleans, I grabbed Sir Lennox and gave him a big hug. I put the jersey on him, stepped back, and smiled. "Promise me you will never give up on yourself, OK?" He extended his pinky, locked it with mine, and sealed it with a kiss. "I promise Daddy." "You promise me too, OK?" I was proud to be affirmative. "I promise Sir Lennox." It was a profound moment for me, and it happened with my family.

The 49ers never signed me back. I continued to work out during that season and then the following one, still nurturing hopes of another opportunity to play in the NFL. However, we did not remain in the Bay Area. Shortly after being released, my family and I moved back to Richmond to begin the next chapter. The pain of those last moments in San Francisco created a resolve. I made a vow amid that experience that I would commit my life's work to helping people find purpose and meaning in their lives. I would challenge others to never give up and I would do everything I could to provide the resources and tools to overcome adversity and recover from life's greatest challenges.

I believe we all have a story that is worth telling. I also believe that when we tell our stories honestly, we can enhance each other's lives. Our existence is more than just having a family, making money, and dying. There is something only each one of us can contribute to the world. Whether our audience is five people, 500, or 500,000, someone is waiting on us to live our truth and contribute our gifts to this world. Our experiences can connect us to our life's work and those we are to encounter along the way. Our failures, setbacks, and tragedies do not have to stop us. As my father-in-law often says, "destiny delayed, is not destiny denied."

What could your symbolic image be? You may never run a football, or even play a sport, but you do have something you value. You have an image of what you could be one day, or maybe you once had a vision of what could be. I challenge you today to revisit those visions. Within them are timeless truths, timeless goodness. Think back to when you were a child, or maybe just graduated from high school or college. Before the opinions of others got in the way and made you hesitate, before you experienced loss and disappointment . . . what excited you then? Don't rush past it or make excuses for it. Let the image of possibility you once held come back into focus. That is what I did when we moved back to Richmond. I had to return to my early sense of possibility without letting it be negated, especially by myself. You must become your own best advocate, not your own worst adversary.

How can this happen? How can you recover, especially, your sense of possibility, the excitement that once motivated you? Start your recovery by taking inventory of where you are now. What is your biggest fear? What excites you? What is important to you? Get a picture to carry in your wallet, place on a wall, or on a screensaver. Something you will see every day. Find something to pull you forward when times get hard, and you want to give up on yourself. It is so easy to lose perspective. Use something outside yourself to bring you back to the possibility that will carry you forward.

The hard part for me was facing fear. What was I afraid of? If football was over. I was afraid of being forgotten. How would I be remembered? I felt like I gave so much yet had so little to show for it. I did not have $50 million accumulated which was the original goal. I had not made the Pro Bowl, won a Super Bowl, or even rushed for 1,000 yards in a season. In reality, I was just another guy. You spend your life fighting to be extraordinary, to excel, to represent endless possibilities to your family, community, and fans. While you are playing you feel this intensely: invincible, rare, one of 1,696 people in the world to be on an NFL team. But when the dust settles and you hang up the cleats, you are one of the 27,000 people who have played in an NFL game. In the end, I would be known as the guy who used to play football. No one cares about used to or has been. In a society of relevance, has-beens are not celebrated. I was afraid of not finding the same passion for life and other interests. I was afraid of starting over. I knew what it took to become an expert in football. Would I have to wait another ten to fifteen years?

Climbing a corporate ladder was not appealing to me and was in fact frightening. Though was it really that different than playing in the NFL? Maybe less glamorous, depending on the company, but the same end result. I was afraid of shifting my lifestyle. I was no longer being paid a professional athlete's salary, which meant my standard of living would need to change. I had bought into an expectation of how I should live, what I should drive, and what I should wear. I was accustomed to taking last-minute flights to wherever I wanted in the off-season.

I had already made the mistake during my first period away from football of neglecting the basic rules of cash flow. What comes in needs to be more, much more than what goes out. When that ratio changes, there is no time for denial; adapt and adjust. I had earned the right to live this lifestyle, I thought. I sacrificed years so that no one could place a limit on how I lived. The possibility of downsizing brought back traumatic experiences of moving from home to home growing up. Felling I was not in control of my future brought a new level of frustration and sadness. I needed to face these feelings.

Then I began having conversations with close friends, advisors, and family members who gave a different perspective. I was reminded of all I had accomplished to get to this point and, more importantly, the impact on others along the way. I was so focused on what I had not accomplished and afraid of what would change, that I was slow to celebrate the accomplishments and the people who have supported me along the way. That was hurtful and demeaning to them. Countless friends, advisors, family, coaches had poured care and guidance into my life over the years. By categorizing myself as a failure, I was devaluing their investments in me. I was too focused on those who do not even know me and what they would think and say. So, wrote down the names of all the people who had influenced me up. My parents, pastors, little league coaches, teachers, friends, advisors, mentors. I became inspired.

I decided I would change my perspective. First, I would be grateful for the experiences I had and the people who supported me. Second, I would learn from the past thirty-one years. I would write down the many lessons I learned. Some would serve me in the next chapter of life and some would be left in the past. In a world where many people do not achieve their goals, I had achieved my goal of playing in the NFL despite the odds against it. As it relates to what I had not achieved, I asked myself and those closest to me, what hindered me from achieving greater levels of success? I identified consistency, mentorship, skillset, burnout, coaching, discipline, and communication in my relationships. These are things I could improve. It was at this moment I determined that football would not be the pinnacle of my life but rather it would serve as a platform. I would carry with me the lessons learned and experiences gained. I would surround myself with coaches, friends, and people who would challenge and support me in this next season of life, and develop the skillsets needed to achieve a greater level of success and ultimately have a greater impact. I felt empowered but where would I start?

Rikki and I returned to Richmond, Virginia because this was home. We needed a support system as we began our transition. First, I wrote down everything that was important to me. When I looked back in the next twenty years of my life, what impact would I like to have? Places I would like to visit, experiences I would like to have, causes I would like to contribute to, information I would like to learn, the lifestyle I would like to live, and relationships I would like to build. I made a promise I would make decisions based off this list and not out of desperation or momentary satisfaction.

Next, I visited the University of Richmond and Episcopal High School. I met with counselors and staff to identify resources and successful alumni from whom I could learn. I made a list of what I wanted to accomplish in this next chapter of life and identified people who have been successful. What former athletes, college and professional, had made successful transitions? What could I learn from reading their stories, following them on social media, and even reaching out to them? Many did not return my call or message, but a few did, and each gave valuable advice which I wrote down and followed.

I was determined to take chances. In football, I learned that I could not play scared, afraid of being hurt, of fumbling, or losing a game. I knew what it felt like to be paralyzed by fear, but I also knew the feeling of liberation and confidence gained through facing it. These lessons took years to learn. I would give myself time to find something I loved and develop the skill to excel in it. I would keep trying even when I failed. I would always keep my goals in front of me and clearly define success. Staying on this journey became one measure.

I also decided to be honest with others and with myself about the help I needed. Some people would judge me, others would be unwilling or unable to help. That was ok. But there would be a few, like the University of Richmond which gave me my only scholarship, or Maurice Carthon who saw enough in me to take a chance in the NFL draft, or Sean Payton, who would give the advice, support, and opportunity I needed. I could not let the embarrassment or fear of rejection stop me from finding those who were there to help. It was hard reaching out and asking for help. Admitting I did not know what to do. When you are used to being perceived as an expert in your field, it is humbling to present yourself as a novice. But that's where I was, and I would not pretend otherwise. I would remind myself of previous lessons learned and remember that this is a starting point, a place from where I can grow. Lastly, I made a promise that I would enjoy the process. I would learn how to have fun. As a kid, football was a game. I excelled because I loved to play. At a certain point, it became a job, a responsibility, which brought stress. I had many responsibilities now as a husband, father, and soon, a businessman. I would find outlets like cooking and regular moments to have fun.

Throughout this journey, I have mentioned the word "faith." What is it? When you hear the word faith what comes to mind? Maybe it is church, a particular religion, a set of rituals or customs, or maybe an idea of who you should or should not be. Some cringe at images of hypocrisy. Faith is what keeps me grounded. It is belief in myself, in something greater than myself, and in a reason for my existence. It is the belief that I am never alone. The belief that when I pray someone hears. The belief that my fears, hardships, and questions are not too big for God. At times growing up, I was told just to believe. Do not challenge God. Just trust what the Bible says. Any good relationship needs time to grow. It was in the darkest times of my recovery, times where I yelled, screamed, cried, and was angry with God that I grew closer.

In these times, I asked these key questions; Why did this happen? How could you let this happen? Why am I here? What is my purpose? Help me to believe. Faith is community, connection. My church community and people I connect with all over this world. I did not always believe in myself or that my life would get better. Church gave me a place for support. More than ever today this world needs hope. As young people and as adults we need role models and examples. We need a support system. I have met mentors in church, father figures, and even lifelong best friends. For me and my family, church is a vital part of being connected to my community. In the busyness of each week, it gives me two hours where I can slow down and remind myself that I am one part of a larger community. It reminds me of the importance to connect with others. We are all going through this life together and trying our best to navigate life's challenges and joys. Throughout my life, I have gone back and forth in what I believe, whether I go to church or not. I have questioned if this idea of God is even real. I think that's natural. I have been through enough to believe God is real. This does not mean I do not doubt or that I do not have days when I question, get lost, confused, or want to give up hope.

I read the Bible, but also enjoy reading and learning about the Qur'an, Torah, and Gita. While I understand and respect that we all have different experiences and beliefs in who or what God is, at the end of the day faith is something you must live and experience. It is not something to be simply read in a book, studied, taught or even something you can fully grasp through a sermon. It does not always make sense, but I do believe in the ideal of "seek and you shall find."

While I have come to my own perspective of what faith is to me, I am glad my parents laid the foundation by taking me to church and teaching me the importance of prayer. A parent's job is to introduce kids to ideas, experiences, and beliefs. My parents gave me a set of core beliefs and values to determine right from wrong and to help me make decisions.

So, define what is important to you. Do not settle or compromise. Find someone you can look up to. Study them, their habits, actions, and words. This is a core part of faith. The path to answers begins with questions.

I say this with all sincerity: I believe in you. I have not met you, yet I believe in you. If you picked up this book and made it this far it means you are already on the journey to becoming the best you can be. I can promise you what you are looking for you will not find in a new job, promotion, new house, or even a relationship. What you are searching for is inside. It is the question of who am I and why am I here? What will I contribute to the world? Will my life have meaning? The answers you are looking for lie in your story, your pain, your fears, the ideas that seem impossible. The causes you are drawn to. The questions you keep asking yourself.

If I have learned anything from football, it has taught me to keep going. Up ten, down ten, put one foot in front of the other. Momentum can change in an instance. Trust your teammates. In football, we had a 24-hour rule. You have twenty-four hours to celebrate the wins and grieve the losses. Give yourself time on this journey. Recovery for some may take months; for others, it may take years. Just keep going. Trust your support team. Ask for help and allow them to help you. Who you become, the lessons learned, and the people you meet along the way are necessary means to completing the story you can tell about your life. My objective in this book is to encourage others to understand and to share their story. It would mean the world to me if you shared your story with me. Let's journey toward recovery together.

Acknowledgments

What do you do when everything you've prepared for is gone? On October 23, 2011, I faced this question. I was the starting running back for the Washington Football Team (then known as the Redskins) of the National Football League when I suffered a torn ACL (anterior cruciate ligament) in my left knee during a game. Over the next four years I faced a lengthy recovery in body and soul. The future for which I had worked was changed beyond imagination.

The story of my recovery from injury can speak to everyone who has been injured or suffered crippling loss. What do you do when everything you've prepared for is gone? Where do you turn? What can you believe? How do you come back? How do you regain hope? This book addresses questions that many people confront. The loss of money, health, close friendships and relationships often follow. How could I come back? How could I find resilience?

In this book, I join with writer William Sachs to tell my story. It begins with the child who had athletic gifts and mental determination. Football took me from a family facing various challenges to a top-flight prep school, Episcopal High School in Alexandria, Virginia, and then to the University of Richmond. Over four seasons I became Richmond's all-time leading rusher and was captain of the team in my senior year. Then the Arizona Cardinals of the NFL drafted me in 2008. My ability and determination were tested as never before. Yet my purpose intensified. I would excel, I would succeed. How I pursued this dream forms the opening chapters of this book. You will get an inside view of the challenges an NFL player faces.

My story reveals the meaning of motivation, adaptability amid hard knocks. It is a story that also describes the journey of recovery, the path to rebuilding my body and my life. I will describe how a rare condition frustrated healing. Yet, after nearly four years out of football, I returned to the NFL for two seasons with the New Orleans Saints. In other words, my absence from football equaled the length of the average NFL career, which is little more than three years. More than returning to the field, I discovered the inner meaning of resilience. This book traces the path of "growth" amid an extended personal trial. I will describe the lessons learned which can guide you toward recovery amid severe challenge. Recovery for me meant becoming stronger and clearer in my determination and my faith. You too can be resilient.

The faith that has defined my life is less about doctrine and more about how one lives, especially how one finds deep purpose. I grew up with the conviction that I could succeed regardless of any obstacles. Deep purpose can guide your life, especially when you face challenge, when faith is tested by unforeseen events. Who you are and what you intend cannot exist simply in your mind. The world intrudes and carefully created intentions can be derailed. I will show how injury reoriented my life and set me on a new course. I never gave up.

For all of us, there is something greater in life, even as we face struggles that threaten all we have known. We can move ahead in ways we never imagined. Renewed purpose becomes possible. Even the reality of injury need not stop us. There is deeper truth. We can be resilient. We can recover to find authentic purpose in the midst of upheaval and struggle.

Numerous people deserve my gratitude. I want to express my thanks to:

Mom and Dad

Coach England and Ron Brown

Jeff Hanson

Pastor Mike and DeeDee Freeman

Pastor Bradley

Charles Maka

Bob Ellis and Aleta Richards

My brother and my sisters

Erica

Eugene Parker

Rich Johnson

Jack and Kim Ross

Dr. Josh Sandell

*Sean Payton, Terry Fontenot, Mickey Loomis
and the entire Saints organization*

Maurice Carthon

Edgerrin James

Brittney Borders

Bridget Johnson

Mr. and Mrs. Jones

Ms. Connie

Rocio Mendizabal

Bill Sachs

Austin Tucker

Nai'lah Rowe

About the Authors

Tim Hightower brings the energy of professional football to the business world. He was a running back in the NFL for seven years. He is the only NFL athlete to return to play after missing four seasons due to injury. Tim is a graduate of Episcopal High School and the University of Richmond. Most recently, he has been a public speaker and provided consultation  to companies on sales, marketing, and health education. Tim excels at building relationships with companies to form business partnerships that meet community needs. He currently serves as the director of alumni relations for the Washington Football Team. He resides in Glen Allen, Virginia.

William L. Sachs is a minister, writer, teacher, and consultant. He has served Episcopal churches in Virginia, Connecticut, and Chicago. He has also served as a foundation vice president and as a visiting professor at Yale Divinity School and Virginia Theological Seminary. Bill has worked in interfaith relations, promoting understanding between Christians and  Muslims in the United States and the Middle East. He is the author or editor of nine books and over two-hundred articles, reviews, op-eds, and book chapters. Bill resides in Richmond, Virginia.

A free ebook edition is available with the purchase of this book.

To claim your free ebook edition:
1. Visit MorganJamesBOGO.com
2. Sign your name CLEARLY in the space
3. Complete the form and submit a photo of the entire copyright page
4. You or your friend can download the ebook to your preferred device

Print & Digital Together Forever.

Snap a photo   Free ebook   Read anywhere

CPSIA information can be obtained
at www.ICGtesting.com
Printed in the USA
JSHW081925190623
43414JS00001B/54